REVOLUTION

of the

HEART

A New Strategy
for Creating Wealth
and Meaningful Change

REVOLUTION

— *of the* —

HEART

Bill Shore

FOREWORD BY
Gloria Naylor

RIVERHEAD BOOKS
New York
1995

Excerpt from "One Way Donkey Ride," copyright © 1975 Jardiniere Music (ASCAP), administered in the United States and Canada by Fairwood Music USA/PEN Music Group, Inc.
Excerpt from "The Cure at Troy" reprinted by permission of the author and Farrar, Straus & Giroux, New York. Copyright © 1990 by Seamus Heaney.
Excerpt from "The Gift Outright" reprinted by permission of Henry Holt and Company, New York. Copyright © 1969 by Robert Frost.
Remarks by Dr. Martin Luther King and Rabbi Abraham Joshua Heschel reprinted from Conservative Judaism *by permission of the Rabbinical Assembly. Copyright © 1968 by the Rabbinical Assembly.*

RIVERHEAD BOOKS
a division of G. P. Putnam's Sons
Publishers Since 1838
200 Madison Avenue
New York, NY 10016

Published simultaneously in Canada

Library of Congress Cataloging-in-Publication Data

Shore, William H.
Revolution of the heart: a new strategy for creating wealth and
meaningful change / by Bill Shore; foreword by Gloria Naylor
p.   cm.
ISBN 1-57322-019-1 (alk. paper)
1. Voluntarism—United States.   2. Civil society—United States.
3. Community development—United States.   4. Human services—
United States.   5. Public welfare—United States.   6. Charities—
United States.   7. United States—Social policy—1993–   8. United
States—Social conditions—1980–   I. Title.
HN90.V64S56   1995   95-35627 CIP
302'.14'0973—dc20

BOOK DESIGN BY DEBORAH KERNER

Printed in the United States of America
1   3   5   7   9   10   8   6   4   2

This book is printed on acid-free paper.

ACKNOWLEDGMENTS

Debbie Shore is the number one reason I was able to write this book and the reason I had something to write about. She started Share Our Strength with me and has been there every day, nurturing it when I was not, and covering my back when my attention was turned elsewhere. It would be hard to ask more from a sister, colleague, and friend. Her assistance to me in revising successive drafts of the manuscript was in character with her decade of commitment to fighting hunger: invaluable.

Many others on the staff at SOS suggested ideas, details, and revisions that vastly improved the book. There are too many to name here, but Catherine Townsend, who has helped to build the organization; Marisa Nightingale; and my assistant, Jason Lonstein, deserve special thanks for pulling together necessary materials and for their insights, enthusiasm, and support.

Acknowledging Flip Brophy, my agent at Sterling Lord Literistic, is like acknowledging a parent in that I simply wouldn't be here without her. At every turn she has been instrumental in launching SOS in new directions. Her commitment to our work means everything to me. Her friendship means even more.

My editor, Julie Grau, is where acknowledgment must yield to admiration and praise. Julie wanted readers to be able to read this book even more than I wanted to be able to write it. To the extent that they can, the credit goes to her. To the extent that they cannot, the fault is mine. There were many times when she understood what I wanted to say more clearly than I did. She gently but firmly coaxed a better book out of me. I can't thank her enough, but I won't stop trying. Assistant editor Nicky Weinstock kept the entire process on track with more warmth and good cheer than an author could expect, and I'm grateful.

The many incredible SOS organizers, volunteers, partners, and leaders around the country are inspiration enough for ten books. They are too numerous to list but their idealism and commitment to ending hunger and poverty make them heroes of mine. They are well represented by Noel Cunningham, Peter Gold, Danny Meyer, Susie Cantor, and Stephanie Crane.

Of my many friends at American Express, John Pritchett, Natalia Cherney, Karen Aidem, and Tom Ryder stand out as best representing the extraordinary partnership between our organizations. They have been generous, caring, committed, and most important of all, willing to share their ideas, experience, and expertise to help Share Our Strength grow. Along with thousands of their colleagues at American Express, they have gone beyond the call of duty to exemplify what citizenship and community can mean in America today.

To those who read and commented on the manuscript—especially Michael J. Rosen and Alan Khazei, who labored over it extensively—my special thanks.

My family, Bonnie, Zach, and Mollie, helped make this book, too. As the poet John Montague wrote, they "lie beneath everything I write; love's invisible ink, heart's watermark."

FOREWORD

There is a childhood parable I remember about a weary traveler who comes to a crossroads and encounters a wise old man. The traveler is looking for a place to rest and inquires of a large town sighted off in the distance: "What kind of people live there?" The old man answers his question with the question, "What kind from whence you came?" When the traveler confides that the last town he visited was full of filthy streets and vicious people, knaves and thieves, the old man tells him, "Avoid that town; it's exactly the same. You will find no peace there." The weary man thanks him profusely for saving him a needless journey and trudges off in the opposite direction. The next day another dusty and tired traveler comes to that same crossroads, meets the same old man, and asks the same question: "What kind of people live there?" But this traveler tells the old man that the town from whence he came was a place of flower-strewn streets, good and giving people who always greeted each other with a smile. And the wise old man says, "The town waiting over the horizon is exactly the same. Go down there and rest in peace."

What kind of America do you live in? Bill Shore tells us that the answer is no further than what rests in your heart. And if we see within the present system only hopelessness over a stubborn resistance to utilizing our wealth and inventiveness to solving poverty and hunger, then we are a country that will always have poverty and hunger. The rich will get richer. The poor will get poorer. And the barriers between them will get larger. We will use our politics to solidify the widening demographics and opposing interests of the haves and have-nots. We will use our wealth to build larger prisons and our inventiveness to manage them more efficiently. That can be one America. It is probably the America that many of us see. But this book offers us the vision of another. Its base is conservative: charitable and social organizations working within the present system, using the wealth of their personal skills to create new wealth through entrepreneurial ventures and partnerships. But its goal is radical: let this new wealth be put to use addressing the immediate and acute need of feeding the hungry along with the long-term need of addressing the roots of poverty. Then we are a country that will see increasing opportunity in reality and not rhetoric. The rich stay rich. The middle class aren't burdened with new taxes. But the poor are able to feed their own children. And those children are able to hope.

Is this man whistling in the wind? Is Share Our Strength yet another bunch of nouveau liberals futilely putting little drops of water in a bottomless bucket of hopelessly tangled social realities? The reality of entrenched power? Of entrenched special interests? Of entrenched racism? Many will think so and for good reason—it's simply not the America that they see. I feel it does little good to argue with such opinions; winning an argument is only to have someone concede a point, it doesn't cause a change of *heart;* and it's through the heart that we see.

As a writer, I belong to a group who sit within the comfort of our studies and cocoons of our minds, observing and unraveling the variegated threads woven into human nature. Too often we see those threads as darker and rather lighter; infused with self-interest; disinterest; even cruelty. There is so much to be done in the righting of the world; and so little effort put to the task at hand. So we warn. We admonish. We rail and wring our hands. But above all, we do care. Or why bother talking about it at all? I love quoting Margaret Atwood, who once said, "People without hope do not write books."

When I was eighteen years old I elected to forgo college and joined a religious sect that preached and lived for the coming of a theocratic government on earth. It was 1968. I was young and idealistic. But it was neither my youth nor idealism that led to the belief that the injustices I saw taking place on the streets of Saigon and southeast Los Angeles needed divine intervention. Reading between the lines of any newspaper or news magazine told me that wars, racism, and rampant poverty were rooted within the systems of our governments and ways of doing business. Pure capitalism as well as pure communism had an investment in the continuing existence of the "have nots." So destroy the systems, I thought, and rebuild from the ground up. The seven years I spent preaching about the coming of a theocratic government that never arrived were not wasted years. Because the bottom line is that I believed this world, not some far-off heaven or nirvana, could be a better place; and I was willing to work for what I believed.

It is 1995. I am middle aged and idealistic. No longer a member of that religion. No longer hoping for divine intervention. It is human intervention that will change the world. We made this mess. We can clean it up. And will we, to any great measure? No, we won't. But it is the small measures that can rule the day. Brick by brick, walls in Berlin, or anywhere else, can come down. Soviet communism sank under the weight of its own rigidity and disregard for personal humanity; and for the same reasons American capitalism will follow behind. Yes, as I see it, the systems are doomed to self-destruct; but that will still leave the people. You. Me. Small measures. Brick by brick.

But for now, the system we have is the system we have. And we can wait for a world revolution while we avert our eyes from the sight of hungry children on our subways, outside our malls, in our neighborhood parks; or we can answer the call for a revolution of the heart simply to *see* another possibility. A new way of doing business in this country. A new way to care. I hope that the level of debate about the philosophy presented in this book will concern itself with those issues. I don't have to endorse every tactic presented here or even think it feasible for some of the grassroots agencies mounting their own efforts against poverty and its cause. But it is indisputable that this book offers us the gift of a simple and powerful vision of a man who came tired and worn to a crossroads and, in spite of the hopelessness of the place from which he came, was determined to see possibility in the place to which he was going.

—GLORIA NAYLOR
Brooklyn, New York
1995

INTRODUCTION

Shortly after my thirty-second birthday, the worst thing that could possibly happen to me happened. At least it seemed that way at the time.

The corporation to which I had devoted my entire professional life suddenly went out of business. Overnight. As swiftly and suddenly as a runaway train jumping its tracks. There was no prior warning. It felt worse than just losing a job. It felt like losing my sense of purpose, my reason for being. I won't go so far as to call what happened a tragedy, though many did at the time and do still.

My job had been my passion. Next to my family, it was the most important thing in my life. The only thing. I had worked at it for ten years, seventy hours a week and almost every weekend. I had prepared for it for five years before that. I had started in the mail room and worked my way up to the top.

The organization's growth from a small, unknown operation to a multimillion-dollar corporation with hundreds of employees had been rapid and impressive by any standard. Eventually it achieved such national recognition that it was not uncommon for our work to make front-page news in the nation's leading newspapers day after day. The job had taken me to forty-seven states where I'd enlisted the help of thousands of people. Most of my closest friends worked with me. My professional and personal life were one. Along the way I'd made sacrifices, and expected the same of others.

Suddenly, one late-night, long-distance phone call from Washington, D.C., brought it all to an end. In the days and weeks that followed, the story of what happened would be repeated over and over again, leading network newscasts and dominating shows such as *Nightline* and *Larry King Live*. The covers of *Time* and *Newsweek* followed suit, prompting obsessive discussion at every cocktail party, summer barbecue, and neighborhood gathering.

The year was 1987. The corporation was called Americans With Hart, Inc. It was the legal vehicle for the 1988 presidential quest of the front-running Democrat, Colorado senator Gary Hart. He was the odds-on favorite to capture the White House that year and to usher a new generation of leadership into power. He stood poised to defeat then–Vice President George Bush and reverse eight years of Ronald Reagan's policies, and to renew and restore the Democratic Party in national politics. His entire career had been that of bold reformer, consistently rejecting and rebutting the conventional wisdom in favor of new and untraditional ways of making politics live up to its ideals.

But Hart's quest, and mine, ended abruptly when he withdrew from the campaign for the presidency in a nationally televised press conference near his home in Denver on May 8, 1987, following reports, as the newspapers came to call it at the time, of his relationship with "a woman not his wife." It was the single most explosive event of modern presidential campaign history. Though I was standing at ground zero when it detonated, I felt not like a victim but rather like an overwhelmed and ultimately ineffective rescue worker.

There are two times in my life I remember crying uncontrollably into unconsciousness. One was in 1978, three days after my mother died suddenly and too young, and I had to leave my father's side in Pittsburgh to return to work in Washington. The other was the afternoon my ten years with Senator Hart came to an end.

On the morning of May 9, less than twenty-four hours after Hart's withdrawal from presidential politics, I woke up in Denver with bloodshot eyes, $9,600 of credit-card debt, no job, and an eighteen-month lease on the house into which I had moved with my wife Bonnie and young son Zach for a campaign that would end after just twenty-one days. I was confused, exhausted, sad, and numb. Later that morning I stepped out onto my driveway and picked up the *Denver Post* and the *Rocky Mountain News*. I stared at the nearly identical full-color front-page photos, and then at the young man with a drawn face and thinning hair standing next to Lee Hart and to the side of the senator as he defiantly announced his withdrawal from the 1988 presidential campaign. As I looked into those sad, anguished eyes, a moment passed before I realized they were my own.

Though I couldn't see it at the time, and wouldn't have believed it if I could, my life was unexpectedly about to change course—both personally and professionally—in the most profound possible way. I had always loved politics and believed in government's power to make life better for people. I'd seen my own father do it in the town where I grew up, and I'd seen it work myself on a large scale in Washington. Most of all, I believed politics and government were the most effective ways to make a mark on the world, to make a difference, to create change. At the time I believed them to be the only way. I was also fascinated by the processes of campaigning, compromising, persuading, and problem solving. They tested you in every way: your intelligence, your agility, your virtue, your integrity, your loyalty, even your physical endurance. I was versed in the biographies of young men—from John Hay in the Lincoln administration to Ted Sorensen in John Kennedy's—who had come to Washington as intimates to new presidents and in their service earned the trust of Congress, negotiated with foreign leaders, and changed the course of history. I aspired to be an heir to that grand tradition, serving anonymously behind the scenes, unelected and unconfirmed, but empowered by the trust and confidence bestowed upon me by the great and powerful men who could count on my loyalty. But that opportunity had been pulled out from under me like a rug, and it would not come back.

Though I would eventually return temporarily to government and presidential politics, I never saw the same promise in either again. My heart and soul would soon shift to another path: one that would enable me not only to maintain my political ideals but to act on them—and enact them—in a more real and meaningful fashion. This chosen course would bring me closer to the people who had inspired me to enter politics in the first place, yield tens of millions of dollars for a good cause, and liberate me to follow my deepest creative impulses and truest desires. Most important of all, I would come to learn that it was a path open not to me alone, but to people with open hearts everywhere, and that by transforming those hearts, it could truly transform society.

❦

Cosmologists know that when a bright star explodes, it scatters seeds that give birth to new universes. But I didn't know that in 1987. I doubt I would have found it comforting if I did. But there were in fact seeds to be gleaned from the experience of nearly ten years of national political organizing at a senator's side. They would soon yield the growth of a new vision, a vision that would change my life, a vision paradoxically beyond politics but at its true core, one that might not change laws or governments, but could change the hearts and minds of those who do.

Today, less than a decade later, that vision lives in the form of Share Our Strength, the hunger relief and anti-poverty organization I founded, which has grown to be one of the largest in the United States. Share Our Strength provides direct financial assistance and other types of support to more than 450 community-based service organizations across the country that help to feed, shelter, teach, and support Americans living in poverty, while also working to prevent hunger in the first place. It supports international relief and development efforts on four continents as well. But Share Our Strength's size and rate of growth are not the point. Impact is. And the reason for that impact is the new way we've engaged people; not by asking them for money, but by asking them to contribute of themselves, through their skills, talents, and most passionate interests, thereby connecting them to their communities in ways money never could. What follows is not so much about the organization Share Our Strength as about what *sharing strength* means, and what it can inspire and create. It is about how this philosophy can be enriching to both the self and the community, how it can be used to reinvent not only our notion of citizenship, but the institutions we rely on to knit our neighborhoods into strong and caring communities.

So far more than $30 million have been raised and distributed by Share Our Strength to help people in need learn to provide for themselves. More important than the money disbursed has been the impact SOS has had on tens of thousands of Americans who have become leaders in their own communities on behalf of the fight against hunger and poverty. Chefs, writers, scientists, artists, musicians, fashion designers, and architects as well as lawyers, accountants, bankers, and corporate executives—many previously uncommitted and uninvolved—have been energized by new and meaningful ways to give back to their community. Some are prominent leaders in their field—chef Alice Waters, author Joyce Carol Oates, singer Stevie Wonder, just to name a few—but the vast majority are unknown, ordinary people making extraordinary contributions, alive to the power of their own individual gifts and literally sharing their personal strengths in ways that support others. Many began by simply participating in a fund-raising event of one type or another, but as their commitment deepened they began to organize events, write articles, give speeches, and form a new generation of activists. As founder of SOS, I helped deliver this infant organization, but it is they who breathe life into Share Our Strength. Their deeds more than my words give voice to this book.

In his autobiography, the great humanitarian doctor Albert Schweitzer wrote: "Judging by what I have learned about men and women, I am convinced that far more idealistic aspiration exists than is ever evident. Just as the rivers we see are much less numerous than the underground streams, so the idealism that is visible is minor compared to what men and women carry in their hearts, unreleased or scarcely released. Mankind is waiting and longing for those who can accomplish the task of untying what is knotted and bringing the underground waters to the surface."

This is a book about untying what is knotted, about tapping the underground waters described by Dr. Schweitzer and bringing them to the surface. It is a book about using that power to create new wealth and change minds and realize possibility. Fundamentally, this is a book about the yearning people have to be connected both to something special inside themselves and, at the same time, to something larger than themselves and their own self-interest. It is a book about how all individuals can give back to their community simply through what they do, through what their creative urges compel them to do. A philosophy of sharing strength does not define a new public policy. Rather it suggests a new way of thinking about our relationship to all public policy, and to those abandoned by our political and social institutions.

And because this is my book, it is also about the journey from traditional politics and activism to a more direct and meaningful way of connecting not only to one's community, but to the people in one's life, indeed to one's self. On that level this becomes a book about meaning, fulfillment, spirituality, and love.

This should not be mistaken for a memoir. My life has been neither long enough nor interesting enough to warrant one. But the journey from thirteen years in presidential politics to the birth of a new model for creating wealth through individual, charitable, and corporate giving has yielded insights for me to draw upon that otherwise might not have been attained.

These ideas cannot be separated from the context of the times in which they were developed. If we are not at a turning point we are at least at a unique moment in contemporary history. America's political institutions, the Democratic and Republican parties, the Congress, the traditional venues for bringing about social change, have been captured by a highly sophisticated political elite whose mastery of polling, negative advertising, fund-raising, direct mail, and other forms of communication and media manipulation must be both admired and feared. The political consultants and technicians of both parties have all but conspired to guarantee that the political system, campaigns, and party functions are closed to all but well-schooled members of the club. They've made it harder for the average citizen, student, businessperson, or entrepreneur to have any significant impact in bringing about change through politics. More tragic than their corruption of the political process is their failure to bring about the real change that they believe to be the end that justifies their means. And even government at its best, along with marketplace forces, offers only a two-dimensional approach to solving community problems that is unlikely to succeed unless the community itself becomes more fully engaged.

It might seem predictable for one who played a major role in three losing presidential campaigns to taste sour grapes and now dismiss politics as an outdated dead end and to embrace instead the private nonprofit sector as a more "pure" alternative to solving major social problems. But that is not where I'm coming from. It is not what I believe. Reforming and revitalizing our political institutions and governmental agencies to make them more responsive and more effective is as important and worthwhile as ever. But given how much is at stake—in our cities, our schools, our environment, for disadvantaged children and families—we can't leave the job to government agencies and institutions alone. It's unfair and a sure setup for failure. Just as we've invested energy and interest and resources in our public sector, we must invest the same in our civil sector to help carry the load. Even if we've never before distinguished the civil sector from the public sector.

I've never really felt I left politics behind, or that my experiences with Gary Hart and Nebraska senator Bob Kerrey, for whom I was also privileged to work, are simply part of the past. Rather, I've tried to take the best of it with me, to a new and different arena. An arena in which people are not organized to promote a candidate or even a cause, but instead are organized to bring out what is best and most creative in themselves, to bring it to the surface on behalf of others. That effort, writ large, can truly transform society because it can transform each and every member of society. It can fulfill the vision of Dorothy Day, the great leader of the Catholic Workers Movement, who said, "The greatest challenge of the day is to bring about a revolution of the human heart, a revolution which has to start with each one of us."

To reach a new level of political effectiveness, to succeed in changing not only the players but the playing field, it will be necessary to bring a new language of community to the table and to create a new vocabulary that gives that language meaning. How can people contribute? What will they use as the bricks and mortar necessary to rebuild their community? What kinds of institutions must be built to serve as a vehicle to get people involved?

Given the size of the challenges facing America on the cusp of the twenty-first century—challenges of poverty, justice, environmental quality, education, and more—neither government, the nonprofit sector, private individuals, nor the rest of society's institutions can, by themselves, effect the kind of changes necessary. It takes more than generals and weapons to wage the kind of battles it will take to change society. It takes more than money. It will take troops. It will take us. And what I couldn't see through the smoke-filled backrooms of American political campaigns I have a better view of now. And that is that millions of people, businesses, organizations, and associations are ripe for the challenge of contributing in new ways, ripe for a revolution of the heart. If this book reaches some of them, one of them, you, it will have been worth it.

REVOLUTION

—— *of the* ——

HEART

1

I hear it was charged against me that I sought to destroy institutions,
But really I am neither for nor against institutions,
(What indeed have I in common with them? or what with the destruction
of them?)
Only I will establish in the Mannahatta and in every city of these States
inland and seaboard,
And in the fields and woods, and above every keel little or large that
dents the water,
Without edifices or rules or trustees or any argument,
The institution of the dear love of comrades.

WALT WHITMAN
Leaves of Grass

In Boston, where harsh winters make heating oil unafford-
able to many poor families, a physician tells me she has ex-
amined children burned by light bulbs their parents used to
try to keep them warm. In Brooklyn, I stand in the cafeteria
with the first- and second-grade students of P.S. 189 who
don't get the free school breakfast they are eligible for and
need because so many chips of lead-based paint have fallen from
the ceiling that the principal closed the cafeteria years ago. A

psychiatrist from Johns Hopkins University debriefs me on his study of the White Mountain Apache reservation in Arizona, where the adolescent suicide rate is a desperate 130 per 100,000 compared to a national average of 11.5 per 100,000. A young teacher at an inner-city elementary school in Washington, D.C., explains that every time she calls parents to invite them to school for a concert, a classroom demonstration, or a conference about their child, the response is the same: "I don't care." Click.

Though spread around the country, these children live in the same place, crowded below the poverty line along with 39 million other Americans. Their crippling situations are not only symptoms of poverty but viruses that perpetuate it. The most important thing I learned in nearly twenty years of working in Washington—and also the most difficult to accept— is that government, by itself, cannot reach or save them. Not because government is bad, too big, too small, or controlled by Republicans or Democrats. But because they need more than what any government can give.

Social scientists who study poverty describe poor children as "at risk." They are not at risk. The risk has already materialized. They are injured. The damage is done. Twenty-seven children die each day from the effects of poverty. Every day more than 846 poor mothers deliver babies at a low birthweight and a high risk of dying before their first birthday. One hundred thirty-five thousand children bring guns to their classroom. More than 2,400 kids drop out of school in America—every day. This is what it means to be poor in America.

I don't expect these statistics to affect you. They may momentarily surprise you but they will not hold your attention. Poverty is so prevalent it has lost its drama. It is not a breaking development to be reported on the evening news, but a long-standing condition; not a leading character on our national stage but the familiar backdrop we no longer notice. The statistics above don't change that perception. They only reinforce it.

Instead of being shocking, poverty has become mind-numbingly routine and ordinary. This makes it all the more difficult to combat. If only there were better odds of poor children being taken hostage somewhere, or stuck in a well, or contracting an incurable disease. The result would be a lot more attention. No one wears ribbons on behalf of the 12 million children who live in poverty.

The child trapped in a well for a week could count on Dan Rather telling the world about her condition each evening. Rescue workers and experts would be flown in from around the country. Neighbors could be relied upon to nurture and sustain the family. Journalists would do special reports on how children get trapped in wells and what can be done to prevent it. Banks, hospitals, local businesses, and other community institutions would respond with funds and equipment. The necessary financial support would be found even though it was not budgeted for in advance. If that child could be saved, she would be saved—because our country has both the resources and the will to save her. But a child trapped in poverty—not for a week, but for a lifetime—enjoys no such outcome. Even if she were the same child that had been stuck in the well. Thirty feet underground, that child is the most visible child in the United States. In plain view on a front stoop in Harlem, that child is invisible. Our nation has the resources necessary to save her. But it does not have the will.

Why not? Why have the billions of dollars spent on promising social programs and welfare assistance not been enough to alleviate either poverty or its suffering? For many families, government assistance programs have been a lifesaving safety net enabling them to put at least some food on the table, avoid homelessness, and afford medicine and other essentials. The alternative could be catastrophe. But at best such programs don't go far enough. At worst they fail to create the systemic change that ensures the next generation will not need the same support. This is not a point of controversy. Liberals and conservatives, Democrats and Republicans, all agree. The status quo has no defenders.

It is tempting to blame government for our disappointment in failed social policy. Those in government give us plenty of reasons. Presidents break campaign promises. Partisan politics keeps Congress in gridlock and needed legislation fails to pass. Politicians study the polls and say whatever they think people want to hear. Powerful special interests have undue influence on legislators and their staffs. Meanwhile schools get worse, violent crime soars, poverty deepens and spreads. This makes government an easy and inviting target. But even if politicians were angels and the political system worked perfectly, it would not by itself assure the change necessary to meet basic human needs in communities across this country. That may explain why even when control of the Congress or the White House changes hands, some of our problems seem intractable. Hard-core poverty, hunger, homelessness, and the existence of an economic underclass stubbornly refuse to yield to either party's tax proposals, economic plans, or educational initiatives. If our efforts to change the way we address social problems are limited to changing government programs, then the cycle of failure will continue. Government is only one piece of what must be changed.

4

If one thing unites Americans of all political persuasions it is the consensus that we need to try something completely different from anything ever tried before to achieve real change.

Think back to the girl trapped in the well. The experts trying to extract her would consider the widest possible range of options to bring her to safety. After trying everything that's ever been tried before, they'd build new structures and try new ideas, even if they were unproven and required a leap of faith. Why? Because a life was at stake. And that life would be so real, so vivid, so tantalizingly within reach that they would not be able to leave and return to their own lives until they'd saved her.

Children in poverty are trapped there. Without help they have as much chance of getting out alive as the girl in the well. Drugs, guns, AIDS, parental neglect, and lack of health care shorten the odds. But instead of creating the widest range of rescue options, only the narrowest and most traditional tools are currently being employed. Anti-poverty policy in the United States is confined to an expensive mix of cash assistance programs for families and children that are generally known as welfare. Americans who live below the official poverty line ($15,141 for a family of four) are eligible for a variety of benefits ranging from basic cash assistance, called Aid to Families with Dependent Children, to food stamps, to Medicaid health insurance. Every year competing Republican and Democratic proposals to reform welfare policy deal principally with how much money is going to be spent on these benefits, for how long, and under what conditions. But those who live and work closest to successful grassroots anti-poverty efforts know that money is not the only issue.

A popular sentiment today is that people are poor by choice. But the convenient and stereotypical image of the "welfare

mother" obscures the millions of working poor in this country—
those who hold down full-time minimum-wage jobs and still
live below the poverty line. Since the modern welfare system
was created, the causes of poverty have changed from economic
conditions, like the Great Depression, to social factors, such as
the breakdown of the family, illegitimacy, drug addiction, and
chronic dependency. Common sense dictates that the remedies
must change, too. They must go beyond economic assistance and
incorporate social factors as well. But they haven't. This is the
principal reason welfare has become hopelessly outdated as a
tool of anti-poverty policy. Welfare needs not only to be re-
formed, it needs to be transformed. It's become a cliché to say we
can't just throw money at social problems, but the so-called welfare reform bills, whether Democratic or Republican, that are
debated in Congress every year do just that, and only that. The
differences are over how much money will be thrown, for how
long, and by whom. Both political parties are so preoccupied
with the levels and structure of financial assistance that they've
failed to look beyond these particulars.

The current approach to welfare perpetuates one of American politics' most enduring and disabling myths: that the key to
fighting poverty effectively is in finding the right formula and
ratio for government expenditures. Even if legislators made all
of the wisest and best choices regarding the key components of
welfare reform—time limits on financial assistance, block
grants to the states, and work requirements for welfare recipients—it would not be enough. It would not give a child a role
model who loves his job, a skill that builds pride and esteem, or
a counselor with advice on everything from homework to fa-
therhood. Those are not things government can mandate,

REVOLUTION *of the* HEART

money can buy, or charity can donate. Instead they depend on whether people who have such strengths are willing to share them.

We can look to political leaders to reform welfare, but to transform welfare we must look in the mirror. Part of the solution must come from within each of us. A commitment to creating change in communities begins with a willingness to change our own lives. Not through higher taxes or more charity, but by giving of ourselves through whatever skills made us strong, by sharing, mentoring, teaching, training, role-modeling, and befriending. So while government deserves plenty of the blame, it does not deserve all of it. Much of the responsibility lies with each of us. Not for causing the problems themselves, but for withholding ourselves, perhaps unknowingly, from the solutions.

The responsibility lies with each of us? How can that be? Most of us are just average Americans, unelected and unappointed to any office, struggling to keep our own lives and families happy and together. We vote, pay taxes, and give generously to charity. Since when have we been expected to play a hands-on role alongside public employees, social workers, and community activists that our tax dollars support? Since when has the success of social policy depended upon our personal participation? Since now. Since the frustrating failures of the last thirty years have proven over and over again that it can't be done without us. We hold the keys to making public policy work.

This does not mean more volunteerism for volunteerism's sake. It does not mean more community service because such service may be good for the soul of the one who serves. It certainly doesn't mean that current Speaker of the House, Newt

Gingrich, is right in suggesting that government can eliminate spending on social programs because charity can make up the difference. Charity cannot. Simple math proves there are nowhere near sufficient resources. To argue that it can is ignorant and creates false and empty choices.

What it does mean is that government programs must be complemented by individual citizens organized and deployed to apply their own special skills and talents on a scale that's never been tried before or even imagined. It means teaching nutrition and food budgeting to young mothers if you are a chef; tutoring math if you are an accountant, coaching if you are an athlete, examining children if you are doctor, building homes if you are a carpenter or builder.

Maybe this is not what you bargained for. Maybe you can't envision how it will work. Maybe the simplicity of the idea strikes you as implausible and naive and reinforces your skepticism and apathy. That's understandable but it only underscores the central point: The disappointing experience of past decades have arrested our ability to reimagine the future. If we can reimagine possibility, it can result in an entirely new vision of how to create lasting change in our communities. Not in a dreamy, wishful, Pollyannaish sense, but rather through a bold and courageous commitment to practical and specific measures grounded in the experience of what has been proven to work over and over again but has not been tried on a large enough scale. Just as in the early days of space exploration, when the future once hinged upon breaking the sound barrier, the future of social policy depends upon breaking the barriers that prevent us from redefining the possible.

One factor that has stood in the way of imagination is government's historic willingness to step in to address social ills when the economy or private market has failed to do so. As a result we have come to accept the illusion that to remedy our social ills we must choose between government or the marketplace or a carefully calibrated combination of the two. But this view is two dimensional, yielding a picture that is flat and misleading. Most of us live, work, play, and raise our families in that space between government and the marketplace. It is in this third dimension where the language of community is spoken that our lives are fullest and most real.

But somehow we are unable to visualize it as a legitimate, serious, and potent force in dealing with staggeringly complicated and frightening social issues. Ironically, as our problems become more complex and seemingly intractable, there seems to be less and less the average citizen feels he or she can do. But this is in fact precisely the signal that citizen involvement and community engagement is indispensable and required. Until we recognize and act upon this fundamental truth, we won't be able to significantly change the social conditions we face.

Michio Kaku, a professor of physics at City University of New York, once explained the role imagination plays in discovering new dimensions. A leader in the debate about the origins of the universe, "superstring theory," and whether there are ten dimensions to the universe, Kaku explained, "The ancients were once puzzled by the weather. Why does it get colder as we go north? Why do the winds blow to the west? What is the origin of the seasons? To the ancients these were mysteries that could not be solved. The key to these puzzles of course is to leap into the third dimension, to go up into outer space, to see that the earth is actually a sphere rotating around a tilted axis. In one stroke, these mysteries of the weather—the seasons, the winds, the temperature patterns, etc.—become transparent."

Likewise when we leap into the third dimension of community in dealing with social issues such as poverty, we'll have a more accurate and realistic understanding of how to deal with issues. In one stroke the mysteries of what we have repeatedly failed to understand will become transparent.

Contrary to conventional wisdom, the fundamental challenge of the day for Americans is not just to make government larger or smaller, make it work better, or reinvent it, though all of those need to be done and we stand to benefit if they are. The challenge instead is to reclaim for ourselves the role in public and civil life we have forfeited. We need to reclaim what we have for too long ignored and neglected: the opportunity for active and meaningful engagement in our own communities. It is the requisite missing ingredient from community-building efforts. Like the dog that didn't bark in the Sherlock Holmes classic, it is the telltale clue to the mystery that has confounded us.

The community dimension is the place with the richest, most accessible, and most effective resources for dealing with community problems. This is where the Boys and Girls Clubs coach after-school athletics, the AIDS clinic treats patients, the revolving loan funds for low-income families operate. This is where the Housing Partnership conducts educational outreach, where the Historical Society develops ethnic-awareness programs, where the Bilingual Multicultural Learning Center sponsors English as a second language classes. And this is where Maternal and Child Clinic pediatricians measure infant growth, where the Lawyers Committee for Human Rights drafts legal briefs, where the Community Violence Prevention Program coordinates violence-prevention programs in the public schools. And this is where entrepreneurial national organizations such as Teach for America, City Year, and Share Our Strength make their mark. An infinite and dazzling array of human services are delivered in and by that community dimension, which exists between government and the marketplace. Unless we give it the weight it deserves, unless we make our political and public policy initiatives three dimensional by including it as an essential part of the solution, government will continue, perhaps unfairly, to bear the brunt of our frustration, and our skepticism of its salience will perpetuate a self-fulfilling prophecy of failure.

☙

It's one thing for someone now outside politics to think beyond government, but it is even more telling when leading political figures begin to embrace and espouse such concepts as well. One of them is New Jersey senator Bill Bradley. For most of his tenure as a senator, Bradley has specialized in developing legislative solutions to such complicated problems as tax reform, international debt issues, and U.S.-Soviet relations. He enjoys a reputation as a thoughtful and serious legislator who thinks before he talks and is pragmatic about pursuing what is possible rather than what is ideal. For the past several years Senator Bradley has been quietly developing his own ideas about the ways to build community, and the role of grassroots "leaders of awareness." In a speech to the National Press Club in 1995, he sought to redefine the role of civic participation on the part of average Americans. Bradley suggests a new and different dimension to the traditional political arguments; in many ways what he is calling for is a philosophy of sharing strength, though those aren't the words he uses. It is particularly impressive that someone from deep within the political structure, with all its built-in blind spots, would have this vision. This is not the way most politicians think or talk. It is worth quoting at length:

> *Our contemporary political debate has settled into two painfully familiar ruts. Republicans, as we know, are infatuated with the magic of the "private sector," and reflexively criticize government as the enemy of freedom. Human needs and the common good are best served through the marketplace, goes their mantra. At the other extreme, Democrats tend to distrust the market, seeing it as synonymous with greed and exploitation. . . . Ever confident in the powers of government to solve problems, Democrats instinctively turn to the bureaucratic state to regulate the economy and solve social problems. . . . These twin poles of political debate—crudely put, government action versus the free market—utterly dominate our sense of the possible, our sense of what is relevant and meaningful in public affairs.*
>
> *What both Democrats and Republicans fail to see is that the government and the market are not enough to make a civilization. There must be a healthy, robust civic sector, a space in which the bonds of community can flourish. Government and the market are similar to two legs on a three-legged stool. Without the third leg of civil society, the stool is not stable and cannot provide support for a vital America.*
>
> *We also have to give the distinctive moral language of civil society a more permanent place in our public conversation. The language of the marketplace says, "Get as much as you can for yourself." The language of government says,*

"Legislate for others what is good for them." But the language of community, family, citizenship, at its core, is about receiving undeserved gifts. What this nation needs to promote is the spirit of giving something freely without measuring it out precisely or demanding something in return. . . .

Above all, we need to understand that a true civil society in which citizens interact on a regular basis to grapple with common problems will not occur because of the arrival of a hero. Rebuilding civil society requires people talking and listening to each other, not blindly following a hero. . . . A character in Bertolt Brecht's Galileo *says, "Pity the nation that has no heroes," to which Galileo responds, "Pity the nation that needs them." All of us have to go out in the public square, and all of us have to assume our citizenship responsibilities.*

As of this writing, Senator Bradley is nearing the end of his third term, and it is interesting to me that he reached these conclusions after sixteen years in Washington, which is precisely the amount of time I've been here and the amount of time it took for me to reach them as well. Of course the difference between being on a Senate staff and being in the U.S. Senate is, as Mark Twain once said, like the difference between lightning and the lightning bug. But still I suppose at least some of our experience was similar. When you first arrive on Capitol Hill, the power and promise of government is irresistibly seductive. The majesty of the ornate marble chambers, deferential guards, and billion-dollar budgets is intoxicating. History remembers and reinforces government's most ambitious achievements, from the

Louisiana Purchase to the New Deal, but has little memory for episodes of impotence. Perhaps government's limitations can't be taught but only revealed and discovered over time, as one sobers. Once they are, the promise and vitality of civil society becomes obvious, logical, and appealing.

When I first started working on a Senate staff in the late 1970s, the political climate was remarkably similar to the one we have today. Elected officials found themselves confronted by a voter rebellion over taxes, government regulation, and government intrusiveness. Californians overwhelmingly approved a statewide referendum called Proposition 13, which radically cut taxes and social services and sent a message that traumatized politicians everywhere. Voters were angry, and in 1980 they proved it by turning to Ronald Reagan, who was elected president on the simple conviction that government needed to be much smaller. Senators, congressmen, and governors panicked. At one point, a constitutional convention to debate a balanced-budget amendment seemed like a real possibility, the first since 1789, notwithstanding the fact that once convened, constitutional conventions must be permitted to debate the entire Constitution and subject any or all of it to amendment. Voters seemed even angrier than they do now, if that is possible, flooding congressional corridors and mailrooms. It was a frightening time. Congress and state governments alike began cutting, trimming, and downsizing and they've been at it relentlessly for two decades with little to show for it.

In the ensuing years, the debate has not been about whether to reduce the size of government (for all intents and purposes, there are no longer many dissenting voices about that), but how. Government is still large. Voters are still unhappy. Both Democratic and Republican presidents have cut billions of dollars and hundreds of federal programs, yet voters are still frustrated, talk radio hosts more strident than ever, and a general feeling persists that the country is going in the wrong direction. The issues and the frustrations are almost identical to what they were decades earlier. Worst of all, after twenty years, the debate over larger or smaller government, more spending or less, has grown sterile and increasingly irrelevant.

If it seems as though we've tried the same things over and over again only to find that nothing works, it's because we have. Actually what we've done is try variations of the same thing. But we seem unable to recognize this. Like a victim of Alzheimer's disease, we are a country whose once-towering strengths have been tragically dissipated by the flight of memory. It's as if we drive around the block, over and over, always surprised and disappointed that we end up in the same place. And while we've spent more and more money to make the trip in bigger cars with better engines, we only get to the same place faster each time, but we do not get anywhere new.

If we tend to invest too much importance in government, then within government we tend to focus almost all of our hopes and energies on the president. In a roundtable discussion hosted by *Tikkun* magazine, Jay Rosen, an associate professor of journalism at New York University, argues that "the most striking development of the current moment is not the faltering of Bill Clinton or an alleged move to the right, but a far deeper problem, the system-wide loss of legitimacy, the surge of antipolitical sentiment . . . to the point where it discredits the entire enterprise of politics." He explains that "part of our task must be to preserve some arena between government and markets, what in Europe they call 'civil society.' We need to help civil society recover its traditions, and its ability to be a counter-voice. We need to recover a civic attitude in our professions, in politics itself, and among young people. It is this civic turn, rather than focusing on the government and particularly on the figure of the president, that might help us navigate the present. We have to stop looking at this rather small figure of the president as the location for politics today."

What makes Senator Bradley's diagnosis so sound to me is not only its effort to reach out beyond the conventional wisdom to find a third way, but its sense of temper and balance. He doesn't scapegoat either government or the marketplace. He hasn't given up on government as a positive force that can change people's lives for the better. He has simply recognized and articulated that some of our problems are bigger than government, and that government alone, government without us, can't solve them. Most Americans aren't really fluent in the language of government or the language of the marketplace, though, like the tourist in Europe, they can make out enough words to get by. But even unwittingly they are fluent in the language of community and that is the language in which their leaders need to begin speaking to them.

As good as it is, though, Senator Bradley's speech goes only so far and then leaves some big questions unanswered. While he declares that "all of us must go out into the public square and assume our civic responsibilities," he doesn't say how. Certainly more citizens must exercise their franchise to vote, but surely we need more than that. More people can call into talk shows or write letters to the editor. But how can people contribute? How can they take the bricks and mortar and rebuild their community? What kinds of institutions must be built to serve as a vehicle for people to get involved?

Examples are emerging every day. College students in New Haven operate a summer camp for inner-city kids—in the inner city. In East Palo Alto, Plugged In introduces disadvantaged kids to computers. The Dallas Area Interfaith brings together churches to set up job-training and after-school programs. In Detroit, Focus Hope offers the disadvantaged training in everything from machinery skills to high-tech engineering. A new magazine called *Who Cares,* "a journal of service and action" was launched to connect young volunteers and activists working for positive social change. All of these efforts are independently organized by community-based entrepreneurs and volunteers who have scraped together enough seed money from private donations to demonstrate the potential of their vision.

There is no shortage of innovative ideas being tried. Social experimentation is rampant. Inspiring success stories exist in almost every neighborhood. But these successes are not enough. They do not lead to revolutionary change. Instead they remain isolated and unrelated instances of achievement that fail to be replicated or expanded. Even the most successful ones lack the infrastructure and venture capital for replication. Success does not guarantee growth or enhancement. Instead, each community is left to fend for itself, create its own efforts.

Senator Bradley says that the language of community is about "undeserved gifts" but he doesn't tell us how to actually speak that language. That's what Share Our Strength and other organizations have been trying to do, to invent a new language of community. This isn't a language that is often heard on Wall Street or in congressional hearing rooms, but it's the language of our kitchen tables, card games, hospitals, and baseball fields. It's our language, and if we don't speak it then it won't be heard.

If we wish to make community problem solving three dimensional, a process in which citizens play a meaningful role in addressing social issues, we must do two things. First, we must support and strengthen the institutions through which they can do so, for the first time in our history, by generating additional resources through the creation of wealth. This will require a profound change in both the attitude and the operations of non-profit organizations around the country. And second, those who are part of the third dimension of community must give more than money, they must give of themselves.

The one compelling reason to do this is that lives are at stake. Not because it fits some textbook vision of good citizenship. Not because it will make us feel better to be good neighbors or return to a kinder, gentler, more civilized time in our history. We need to do this because the lives of children literally depend on it. The survival of at-risk children, families, indeed entire communities, depends upon whether we can begin to demonstrate both the imagination and the courage to put ourselves into the mix of ingredients that are indispensable to making social programs work, and to do it in a way and on a scale that has never been attempted or even imagined. More tragic than even the poverty itself is the legacy of inaction we are leaving our children. Adam Walinsky, a lawyer and activist who has studied the soaring rates of violence in America and helped to create the legislative basis for a corps of citizen police, wrote in the *Atlantic Monthly* that the worst lesson we're imparting to the next generation is, "We will do almost anything not to have to act to defend ourselves, our country, or our character as a people of decency and strength. We have fled from our cities, virtually abandoning great institutions such as the public schools. We have permitted the spread within our country of wastelands ruled not by the Constitution and lawful authority but by the anarchic force of merciless killers. We have muted our dialogue and hidden our thoughts. . . . We have become isolated from one another, dispirited about any possibility of collective or political action to meet this menace."

Time is not on our side. The economic and social landscape is rapidly changing. The forecast is for a mud slide. Every day poverty deepens and becomes more concentrated. The increase in the number of Americans living in poverty is growing at a rate three times as fast as the population as a whole. Between 1980 and 1990 the number of people living in areas of concentrated poverty nearly doubled, rising from 5.6 million to 10.4 million. Today the least affluent 20 percent of Americans earn only 3.6 percent of the nation's household income, while the most affluent 20 percent earn 48.2 percent. In Washington, D.C., capital of the richest nation in history, where infant mortality rates are twice the national average, half of all children live in poverty, twice the proportion just five years ago. The issues are not just economic; they are social. One statistic that speaks volumes about the breakdown of family, neglect, isolation, and despair in our lowest-income communities is that today the leading cause of death for black children aged one to four is fire.

Again, statistics. And again, they inform but they do not compel. Statistics come from research organizations. They don't belong to anyone's family, they are not a part of anyone's neighborhood. The child trapped in the well is. She is real and we can go to her. We can rescue her. In the past we always have. The child trapped in poverty is real too, part of someone's family and someone's neighborhood. We can go to him. In the past we have not. We've sent money, and social workers, and government bureaucrats. We haven't gone ourselves. Probably because it means going into neighborhoods where we've never been, or because we wouldn't know what to do once we got there, and even if we did we wouldn't have the resources to accomplish anything. But a new road map can take us there. A reimagined sense of possibility can provide the faith to make the journey.

2

No one is given a map to their dreams
All we can do is to trace it.
See where we go to, know where we've been
Build up the courage to face it.

SANDY DENNY

My father's name was Nathaniel Shore but almost
everyone called him Nate. The few who didn't, who
called him Nushie instead, gave themselves away as
boys he'd grown up with in Pittsburgh's poor Hill District.
From the time of my birth in 1955 until I began law school in
Washington twenty-two years later, my father ran the district
office of our local congressman, Representative Bill Moorhead.
The office was located downtown, in the new federal building

across from U.S. Steel's towering rust-girded skyscraper. My earliest impression of the federal government's power and largesse was formed by the fast, ear-popping elevators and the well-stocked supply cabinet my dad let me pilfer during visits. Shelves of tablets, pens, staplers, folders, even ashtrays—each and every one emblazoned with the official seal of the House of Representatives more than two hundred miles away. As we'd come and go my father would greet the paperboys and security guards by name, and I'd marvel at the mystery of his having these unusual friends I'd never heard of or met.

Dad managed the congressman's campaigns, organized his visits to the district, advised him on the local impact of legislative issues, answered his mail, and met with all those in Pittsburgh who needed to see their congressman. In those days, working-class voters from a steel town like Pittsburgh didn't belong to lobbying associations or travel to Washington. There was no C-Span or CNN on which you could see your representative. You saw your congressman when he came home to you, which at that time was not very often. Or you saw his assistant. In Pittsburgh, you saw my dad.

Congressman Moorhead was a traditional liberal Democrat of considerable personal wealth. Born to privilege and sent to private schools, Moorhead learned much from his father, the legal counsel to the Mellon family, which had built a banking and philanthropic dynasty in Pittsburgh during the heyday of the steel industry. He was a man who tried to do the right thing and usually did, compiling a distinguished legislative record, which included helping to author the Freedom of Information Act, banking reforms, and a variety of environmental safeguards. His House seat, like every office with a Democratic incumbent in Pittsburgh at that time, was safe from serious opposition so long as he maintained the favor of organized labor's powerful unions. He did. One of the political legacies of Franklin Roosevelt's New Deal was a Democratic Party "machine" in Pittsburgh that, as in Chicago, Buffalo, and a handful of other industrial cities, completely controlled the local political infrastructure. Moorhead was a "machine candidate," a term used with pride, not opprobrium. Once the bosses anointed him, there could be no opposition. In Pittsburgh the Republican Party was a party in name only. TV spots in congressional elections were unnecessary and nonexistent. The most aggressive campaign tactic my father employed was handing out red-and-blue key chains with Moorhead's name and picture on them. When there were extras I took pocketfuls to school, where they were prized possessions among my classmates, though not one of us carried a key.

Moorhead's infrequent trips to Pittsburgh were a whirlwind of handshakes and, "Nice to see you, nice to see you." My dad was always at his side, whispering the name of whoever was approaching, or when there wasn't time, making introductions laced with clues like, "You remember Dave Speisak from East Liberty, don't you, Congressman?"

"Of course I do. Nice to see you, Dave. Nice to see you."

Congressman Moorhead was a handsome man, whose carefully groomed silver hair reflected wealth and breeding. But his pinstripe suits and Brooks Brothers rep ties looked as out of place in Pittsburgh's union halls as bowling league shirts would have on his yacht. My dad had been with Moorhead since his first day in office, and had been with Moorhead's predecessor for two years before that. They couldn't have come from more different backgrounds but they shared two things: a faith in activist government's ability to help people and a wrinkled gray trench coat that my father kept in the trunk for rainy days. Moorhead had a residence in Washington's tony Georgetown neighborhood near the town house Senator John Kennedy occupied. He also leased a converted garage in the Shadyside section of Pittsburgh. You can guess where he spent his time.

Friends and neighbors joked that my dad *was* the congressman. And while he never cast a vote in the House of Representatives or even had his name in the newspaper, I remember how the simplest trip to the Morrowfield pharmacy or Minneo's pizza parlor could take more than an hour or two for all the people who stopped him to ask about getting an uncle into the Veterans Hospital, or a son into the naval academy, a fiancée's immigration papers, or a lost Social Security check. He never wore a watch and was never in a hurry. His cheerfulness was unforced and he had the relaxed manner of one who, if not wealthy in money was at least wealthy in time.

I'd fidget restlessly, pluck or twirl shiny products from store shelves, and whisper with an eight-year-old's impatient urgency, *"Dad,* c'mon, the pizza is gonna get *cold,* c'mon, *c'mon."* But while I fidgeted, I listened, less to the words, which of course I don't recall now, than to the tone of my father's voice: soft, comforting, reassuring, and above all, patient. Whatever the problem, he'd seen it before and could put people at ease. He was the doctor who knew the fever would come down, the shopkeeper who could order more and have them in a few days. "Don't worry. I'll check into it. It should work out. Call me at the office on Monday." His petitioners, especially the old and worried ones, always wanted to tell their tale twice, grasping his elbow or shirtsleeve to buy more time, to lend more detail, to relay a friend or neighbor's suggestions. It was more than he needed to know. But he listened and listened more. "Call me Monday. At the office. Call me Monday." There was nothing he couldn't fix within the week.

When we'd get back home my mother would ask with exasperation, "Where have you been? How could a pizza take so long? It's been almost two hours!" He'd be whistling or singing off key as he put things away in the kitchen, and then he'd sit right next to her on the couch in our living room, hold her hand, and tell her whom we had met and what they wanted and what he was going to do about it when he got to the office. I'd roll around on the floor and listen to the whole thing for the second time. He never gave the impression that he was doing someone a favor. It was more as though their problems had become his problems, and so of course he needed to solve them. I grew up believing that what connected people to the help they needed was my father.

❦

Five-thirty was the latest Dad ever walked through the door, and that was only if the bus that dropped him at the corner of Alderson and Tilbury streets was fifteen minutes late. My mother, Bryna, would lie curled in her robe on the living room couch waiting for him, eyes closed but ears perking up like a puppy's when she caught the sound of the bus's grinding gears half a block away. She had worked as a secretary at the Veterans Administration until I was born, but then stayed home until my sister, Debbie, and I were grown. For a brief period after that there would be a number of attempts at part-time or full-time work, but by then, in her late forties, a good match was hard to find and they all seemed to end in disappointment.

Her whole life she suffered from what she called "nerves." My father called it anxiety. I now know it was depression. It was severe enough after my birth to be considered a nervous breakdown. Her own childhood had been harrowing. She grew up poor, raised by recent immigrants. Her father was often absent from the family when she was a small child, and then died in an asylum before she was nine. Her older brother, Bill, for whom I was named, filled her father's place, but too briefly. He survived World War II, only to be killed in a horrible collision with a truck a few miles from his home. My mother never fully recovered from his death. Their sister, my Aunt Audrey, who lived in the apartment next door with two young children of her own, fed, changed, and raised me until I was two. I have no memory of this, of course, but I've long overheard bits and pieces whenever our family gathers for a holiday meal, graduation, wedding, or funeral. The details remain blurred, and just as staring at an Impressionist painting won't bring the lines and spaces into sharper relief, the overall shape and form is nevertheless clear.

While growing up, we never considered our mother to be sick. I've never felt consciously deprived by her incapacitation. She conserved what energy she had for her children, always wanting us up on the couch with her, to hear about our day, to brush back my hair, press her lips to my forehead, and murmur lovingly in Yiddish, *"Schoen vie die welt,"* which I discovered in high school German meant "as beautiful as the world." She was mother to the rest of the kids in the neighborhood as well, organizing kickball games and popping popcorn or whatever else it took to keep children at close range. Teenagers came to her for advice about their parents, and parents came to her for advice about their teenagers. She dispensed all of it with a genuine cheerfulness but kept none of the cheer for herself. Between her and my aunt, I suspect I benefited from two mothers' love. When my mother's health improved, both of our families moved into houses just eight doors apart, on the same side of the same street, about a block from the old apartment building. Thirty-six years later my sister and I still own our house. Audrey, widowed ten years, still lives down the block, alone, in hers.

The eight hours my father was at work each day were desperately long for my mother. She'd watch TV, read, or talk on the phone to her girlfriends, who were almost always her cousins and who all lived within the same few blocks of our tight-knit Jewish neighborhood. By three in the afternoon, drained of all energy by depression's toll or prescription drugs that seemed to have the same effect, she'd lie like a wilted lilac that could be stirred only by the fresh, promising breeze my father seemed to bring home with him. After school, I'd play with my toys on the living room floor so she wouldn't be alone. Even the brief moments it took for Dad to get from the corner to our house in the middle of the block were too long for her; perhaps they seemed the longest of all. She would wiggle two fingers between the ivory slats of our Venetian blinds, waiting to get a glimpse of him. When at last he turned up our walk, his familiar whistle an answered prayer, Mom got up to kiss him, get dinner from the stove, and we would all take our seats at a little booth in the kitchen's nook, a space that seems impossibly small today, as if built for a smaller race a thousand years ago.

I sat on my dad's side of the booth, against the wall, across from my sister and my mom. While Mom popped up and down getting things from the stove, fridge, or counter, Dad would talk about his day, whom he met, had lunch with, spoke to on the phone, and what their problems were. Senator Romanelli might have helped with a scholarship. Someone he and my mom had both worked with at the Veterans Administration, where they had met years before, might have won a promotion. In turn, my mom would catch him up on the family news of the day. Cousin June's asthma was worse. Cousin Glor was having her house painted and the painter offered to do ours for the same price. They'd take turns, back and forth like this, interrupted often by my sister and me asking who and what and why and how. The mealtimes of some families are marked by long silences, but this was never the case in our home.

If it were a spring or summer evening we'd move out to the front porch afterward, and neighbors from up and down the street would come to talk politics with both my parents, who received deference as local experts. They had heard my dad speak of meetings with the mayor and the governor. They'd seen Congressman Moorhead in our car and at our house. Kennedy, Johnson, Hubert Humphrey were all heroes. And of course none was greater than Franklin Roosevelt. Dead ten years when I was born, he seemed like a figure from the distant past, but on my front porch he was still alive, as he was in my parents' recollections of his voice, his radio addresses, and his legislative victories.

Squirrel Hill was a modest working-class neighborhood: butchers, carpet and siding salesmen, shopkeepers, and city employees. All were first-generation American Jews whose parents had come over by boat in time to bear sons old enough to fight in World War II, and daughters who would remember forever those years without the men. Nearly every family except ours went to synagogue regularly. But ours was not an observant household. As I grew older and approached thirteen, it became clear to the other boys that I was not going to have a bar mitzvah, and they resentfully teased that I was not a good Jew. When I told my parents, they explained to me that instead of sending me to temple or Sunday school they were going to teach me to be a good person and a good neighbor. If they succeeded, they explained, I would not only be a good Jew, but I'd know what was most important to all of the world's religions.

The houses on our street were small and lined up in a neat row, with maybe six to eight feet between them. Our house, red brick with three small bedrooms, was right in the middle of the block. If all the neighbors on either side of us kept their awnings up, which they usually did, then you could see through each family's front porch, with a kind of telescoping effect, all the way to the corner. The steel mills of Jones & Laughlin, which brought prosperity and then pollution to Pittsburgh, seemed far away, but in reality were no more than a short walk around the bend to the river, shooting flames into the sky that could be seen from our home. The sky was black overhead but forever orange on the horizon.

Alderson Street itself was a safe playground, with little traffic and a handful of parked cars that might go weeks at a time without being moved. We used them as goal lines, bases, or hiding spots, except for the Rambler that belonged to Mr. Handleman, who sat on his porch for what seemed to be the sole purpose of guarding the sedan. If anyone came within ten feet of it, his old-country voice boomed: *"Stay avay from da machine!"*

While the grown-ups sat smoking and talking politics and sports, or catching up on neighborhood gossip, the kids would play in the yard, by the telephone poles made sticky with oozing black tar, or in the narrow lane between the houses: kickball, tag, army, tug-of-war, construction crew. None of us could make out our parents' words, or even cared to. But from below the porches, looking up at the haze of smoke or scrunching our faces in disgust at the long strips of speckled flypaper, the soft murmurs of our parents seemed to blend into one long, low-grade hum—a reassuring harmony to young ears, like God exhaling a deep breath. The pungency of boiled cabbage poured through Mrs. Davis's kitchen window and wafted up the block. Frank Sinatra eased out our windows, "The Summer Wind" playing over and over through living room speakers that my mother moved flush against the window screens.

Our family never took a summer vacation together, but we didn't feel deprived because we didn't know any other family that took one, either. To think that a mere ten to fifteen years earlier virtually every one of our fathers had been slogging through Pacific jungles or liberating European concentration camps. This quiet, safe little street, with its sounds and smells and hum, must have seemed like a vacation all the time.

The one family trip we did make was to Washington in 1968 to join in a large protest march against the war in Vietnam. The streets were clogged with hundreds of thousands of demonstrators. The hotel we were to stay at had lost our reservations and kept us waiting for nearly an hour. There were long lines at the registration desk and the lobby was swamped with young ragged-looking protesters with nowhere to stay and nowhere they could afford to stay anyway. The clerk at the registration desk looked harried. My father kept saying, "That's okay. Take your time," and was ultimately rewarded with an upgrade to a three-bedroom suite by a hotel manager grateful for his patience. My mother used the time to do something the hotel could not possibly have foreseen and did not appreciate: shop for groceries and make peanut-butter-and-jelly sandwiches for the hungry-looking college kids who were milling around the lobby.

We stayed in Washington for three days. It was long enough for me to fall in love with the broad boulevards and gleaming white buildings, though most were protectively surrounded by National Guard troops and closed to the public. Around every corner, organizers with bullhorns instructed contingents of protesters as they disembarked from long bus rides. Placards and buttons of every shape and color abounded. ANOTHER MOTHER FOR PEACE. ALL WE ARE SAYING IS GIVE PEACE A CHANCE. I began a futile attempt to collect one of each but had to abandon it once the first shoe box was full. From every state there were marchers, veterans, students, priests, laborers, nurses, college professors, and others taking to the street to compel an entrenched government to change a policy it did not want to change. And it was working. Even a thirteen-year-old could feel the exhilaration of average Americans trying on the cloak of citizenship and finding that it fit. Like a child on her first bike ride without training wheels, people detected a new sense of balance in their lives. Hundreds of thousands of people from every corner of the country—complete strangers—smiled and greeted one another and helped out where they could with a neighborly familiarity born of this common bond.

Each morning I woke before my parents, snuck out of the

hotel room, and walked the few blocks to either the White House or the Capitol while the streets were nearly empty and quiet. I'd stand as close to the buildings as I could get and stare and stare, curious about the few anonymous officials who would come or go. Were their briefcases stuffed with classified documents? Would they be preparing a briefing for the Speaker of the House? Would they end the day in a committee chairman's mahogany-paneled hideaway with bourbon and cigars? I'd try to imagine what important business brought them to the buildings at this hour and whether they were allied with or against those of us on the street. I went back to Pittsburgh eager to return and see the buildings from the inside.

❦

The phone rang day and night at our house. The one phone, mounted firmly on the kitchen wall, that you could take your time to answer without having to race an answering machine that might pick up instead. Occasionally Congressman Moorhead called from Washington. If I answered, I'd try to remember every word of our brief conversation so I could pass on this brush with history to anyone I saw that day. But usually it was more routine. Someone from the north side wanted the snow plows to come to her street faster. Somebody in East Liberty wanted to get his mother a better hospital room. A graduate student at Carnegie-Mellon needed to get his loan extended. Not the stuff of which great public policy debates are made or nations realigned, just the small everyday incidents in people's lives that leave them happier or sadder, optimistic or discouraged, secure or insecure. This must be what my father loved doing, for he did it for years, friendly and patient, without complaint or pretense.

The history of local politics in post–World War II America is filled with places and times where the ability to get such things done would make a man like my father a power broker, one to fear or curry favor with. Such an ability would have put him in the position to receive perks and extract favors of his own. I suppose Pittsburgh in the late fifties and sixties actually was such a place and time, but he was not that kind of man.

After serving for four years in World War II, my father had gone to law school at night at Duquesne University (as I later would at George Washington) on the GI bill, and worked days at the Veterans Administration, where he met my mother. Four years at war seemed like an incredibly long time, and I remember asking him about it when I was a teenager.

"Being in the army four years must have been tough, but I'll bet a lot of good things came out of it, too, huh, Dad? I'll bet you, like, learned a lot of stuff?"

"No, not really. It was just four years. I can't think of anything good about it."

I asked the question that all boys ask of their soldier fathers. "Did you ever kill anyone?"

"I hope not," he replied.

"He shot at trees," my mother volunteered.

He had no adventurous war stories. No war buddies that he looked up or hung out with, either. On the surface at least, the war appeared to have only two lasting consequences for him: He could not drink rum and didn't like to even hear the word (he'd drunk too much crossing the choppy Atlantic on the *Queen Mary* when he returned from Europe in 1946). And he could not watch *White Christmas* without getting choked up.

Like many others, he had either left the war behind or kept

it crammed into a dusty green duffel bag in a locked room in our basement. Helmets with swastikas. Daggers in jeweled sheaths. Tattered copies of *Stars and Stripes* magazine. Stacks of letters bound with rubber bands. Once I dragged it all upstairs into the living room. My mother shrieked: "Oh, that stuff is horrible! Get it downstairs!" My dad barely looked up.

He was the most unpretentious man I've ever known. He never sought to make hard tasks look easy or to make easy ones look hard. At home or "up street" (which meant the butcher shops and bakeries of Murray Avenue), he almost always dressed in a plain white T-shirt and a pair of khaki pants with a crumpled hanky hanging out of the back pocket. His hair was white for as long as any of us could remember; he insisted it had turned that way at eighteen, when he received his draft notice. He was forever blowing his large bumpy nose, broken four times: first when his brother knocked over his cradle, then by a falling bunk in the army, and twice in sports accidents. Babies and young children couldn't resist grabbing onto that nose, which he made easy by always being on their level, quick to smile and clap his hands together, sitting or lying on the carpet whenever kids were about, letting them swarm over him, the other adults inaccessible on sofas or at the dining room table.

When he got a car he picked up strangers at the bus stop and gave them rides downtown, something unthinkable in this day and age. And because Aunt Audrey's husband was disabled and she didn't drive, he chauffeured her family of four everywhere: grocery shopping, doctor's appointments, school plays, whatever. In those days a Plymouth Fury or a Chevy Impala was large enough to hold all eight of us, and there were at least two weeks every summer when we all drove back and forth each day the fifteen miles to the Blue Spruce swimming pool. Both my mother and her sister would fret anxiously over the danger posed by each passing truck, pleading with my father to let the eighteen-wheelers pass, as if they were terrifying prehistoric beasts that needed to be pacified.

If the pressure of all the phone calls, the favors, and my mother's precarious and increasingly dependent state of emotional health ever got to him, it never showed. As I grew older I used to watch him more and more closely, secretly scrutinizing his face and eyes for any sign that he might be sagging under the burden. Except for an occasional martini too early in the day, there were none. When my mother died young and suddenly at the age of 54 in 1978, the muscles of her heart worn out by too many prescription drugs and by the uphill race from whatever demons pursued her, I learned that only tragedy could upset Dad's marvelous sense of balance.

My father was an educated and well-versed man. Though I can't recall him holding a book, I can't recall him not holding a newspaper. He read every section, no matter how long it took, and when he finished he folded it to the crossword puzzle and he and my mother would take turns with it, shouting questions to each other from whatever parts of the house they were in. From the time I was born he never worked a weekend or spent a single night away on business, except for August 23, 1963, the day he stood in a crowd of over 200,000 beside the reflecting pool at the Lincoln Memorial listening to Martin Luther King tell the world that he had a dream. I never heard Dad speak about public service, community, the public interest, or any of the terms so in vogue today. But I did hear a lot about Mrs. Piper's unemployed brother, Mark Chernoff's client, Dr. Silverbloom's patient. He never pronounced any lofty philosophy of life, but he had a rule for navigating Pittsburgh's steep icy streets in winter and they may have been one and the same: You can get anywhere you want to go if you just take your time.

There were no dramatic moments in our family history, no lectures or heart-to-heart talks, no turning point at which he took me aside to impart some important lesson about life. Instead there were lots of corny jokes, bad puns that made all of us slap our hands to our heads and moan, "Oh, Dad!" and, more than anything else, a day-in and day-out example of being there—for our mom, for my sister and me, for anyone who called or bumped into him and needed help. I can't recall his ever trying to influence my career or the path I chose for myself, though I know now that no one influenced me more.

Instead of applying pressure, he supplied opportunity, like the chance to serve as an intern in Washington during my junior year in college with an environmental oversight subcommittee, which Congressman Moorhead chaired. Squeezed behind a desk in an inner corridor between offices in the Rayburn House Office Building, I read and summarized committee reports, attended and reported on hearings, learned how to sit still for eight hours a day, and observed firsthand the role and control that congressional staff had in government. The six-month internship flew by and only whetted my appetite for more. I went back to school knowing that the day after I graduated from college in Philadelphia in May 1977, I'd return to D.C. for a job in government.

———◆———

3

Nothing that is worth doing can be achieved in our lifetime;
therefore we must be saved by hope. Nothing which is true or
beautiful or good makes complete sense in any immediate
context of history; therefore we must be saved by faith. Nothing
we do, however virtuous, can be accomplished alone; therefore
we are saved by love. No virtuous act is quite as virtuous from
the standpoint of our friend or foe as it is from our standpoint.
Therefore we must be saved by the final favor of love which is
forgiveness.

REINHOLD NIEBUHR
The Irony of American History

Nearly ten years have passed since the turmoil that rocked American politics, my family, and my job in 1987. To some, former senator Gary Hart's political career seems like ancient history today, hardly fertile territory from which to draw inspiration or public trust. Hart built his formidable grassroots political organizations on the talents of idealistic twenty-three-year-old organizers whom he championed, but a twenty-three-year-old today would have been twelve when Hart stunned the nation with his first upset victory in the 1984 New Hampshire presidential primary. It was a triumph that catapulted him onto the cover of *Time* magazine and into the consciousness of a new generation of political activists. But most recent college graduates today have only the dimmest memory of who Gary Hart is, and that memory is confined to 1987 and his departure from politics, not what he accomplished during the two decades before that. My story is not about Hart, or what happened to him, but the journey began there and influenced my development and that of Share Our Strength in more ways than I can count. The way his presidential ambitions ended doesn't change that. Hart may no longer be a politically fashionable role model but the lessons I learned by his side were good ones that stuck with me.

Profiles of Hart in *Time* and *Newsweek* caught my eye when I was still in high school and he was managing Senator George McGovern's 1972 presidential campaign, and then two years later, when, in his first bid for elective office, he defeated an incumbent and won a U.S. Senate seat in Colorado. I graduated from the University of Pennsylvania in 1977, determined to go to Washington and work for him.

Congressmen and senators could make laws and those laws could help people. It never occurred to me at the time that even the best legislative efforts sometimes missed the mark, or that even when they didn't, government intervention alone might not be enough to create the long-term changes that people or communities need. But nine months in Washington, even as a naive and impressionable college student saddled with an intern's "gofer" chores, was long enough to see that some legislators were show horses, others workhorses; some were there for the ride, others for a purpose. Hart struck me as serious of purpose, but also as bold, unconventional, and headed for bigger things.

I volunteered as an intern in Hart's Senate office hoping to get noticed and put on the payroll. In truth I probably would have paid for the opportunity to stay. Just walking the few blocks from the Union Station subway to the Russell Senate Building made it all feel worthwhile. If I took my eyes off the bright white Capitol dome it was only to daydream about august debates and great leaders who once labored there. Nearly every day I was sent to the Senate document room near the Rotunda on the Capitol's second floor to retrieve recently introduced bills or resolutions. Waiting patiently while the document clerks climbed ladders to reach old wooden sliding drawers stuffed with freshly printed bills, you couldn't help but look around and think that for all that was wrong or superficial or even corrupt with politics, at its core were ideas—drawers and shelves and mountains of ideas, large and small, about how we as Americans, as human beings, care for ourselves.

Over the course of four months, as my meager savings evaporated, I turned down two job offers on the House side in the hope that something with Senator Hart would materialize. I often hoped Hart would materialize. An intern rarely sees the senator he works for. Instead the senator remains a mysterious, awe-inspiring figure whose decisions, commands, and wishes are conveyed by his administrative assistant or scheduler. I never went anywhere near the senator's personal office or the office leading to it. For much of my internship I was stationed across the street in an old apartment building that had been converted into a congressional annex and was filled with typists, secretaries, other interns, and a few obscure congressional commissions.

Finally, just as my finances dwindled dry, the person who opened the mail in Hart's office left. I got the job and six months later was even permitted to answer some of the correspondence. Over the next ten years I moved through all of the other jobs in the office: legislative assistant, speechwriter, legislative director, and finally, during the presidential campaigns, political director.

It wasn't until 1982, when Hart quietly began to prepare to run for president, that our relationship deepened and changed. A paradox of presidential ambitions is that those who hold them are initially too shy to confide them, even to those with whom they are close. It is such an audacious, presumptuous, preposterous thought—that one is ready to be president—that it is often left unsaid. Instead potential candidates and their family, staff, and friends talk about it elliptically, or in code, or at best hypothetically, until it becomes a fait accompli.

One morning after breakfast in the Senators' Dining Room with a guest who updated him on New Hampshire politics, Senator Hart turned to me and said, "You ought to go up to New Hampshire sometime just to see what's going on." I was shocked. First, Hart had not discussed with me or anyone whether he was planning to run for president. Even among his senior staff there were strongly differing opinions about his intentions. Second, Hart knew a legion of better-qualified political organizers from the McGovern campaign, whereas my political career had been limited to handing out Congressman Moorhead's key chains to friends in junior high school. Nevertheless it was an overture to move to his campaign if there was going to be one, so I seized it.

Within a few days I was making the nine-hour drive to New Hampshire in my Renault Alliance to learn which Democrats might be interested in Hart, what local issues were controversial, and to develop contacts and supporters. It was a trip I was to make about every ten days for the next eighteen months. At Hart's insistence we recruited a completely indigenous field operation, relying not on out-of-state political operatives with impressive national reputations, as did the rival campaigns, but instead on regular New Hampshire residents—mothers, teachers, salesmen, lawyers, and the like—who believed in our cause and would become activists on its behalf. They came to feel more invested in the effort than professional campaign organizers ever would, and because they were fresh and new to this type of activism, their energy had not been drawn down. Their batteries were fully charged.

Ten days before he won the New Hampshire primary, in a chaotic moment where staff and Secret Service agents and press and supporters were jostling for his attention and shouting conflicting directions, Hart turned to me in desperation and said, "You better stick next to me from now on to keep things sorted out." I took him at his word. I stayed at his side virtually every day from then until he left politics.

It was a steep learning curve, ranging from the formal rules of Senate procedure and the informal folkways of the institution, to the minutia of domestic and foreign policy debates, and the rigors of a primary campaign schedule that often consisted of events in four states a day. There were many teachers to learn from and admire, but there was only one headmaster, and that was Hart.

❧

The end of those ten years came with a phone call to my home in Denver at about 10:00 P.M. on the night of Saturday, May 1, 1987. My wife, Bonnie, and my not-yet-two-year-old son,

Zack, were asleep in the back of the house. I had just come from his room, where in the shadows cast by his night-light it was my habit and neurosis to stand quietly, hand stretched softly over the colorful dinosaurs on the back of his pajama top, until I could feel the reassuring rise and fall of his breath.

Gary Hart was calling. He'd announced his second campaign for the presidency just two weeks before, on April 17. It had been a rocky two weeks. The announcement itself, made while standing on a flat rock alone against the wintry Colorado mountains in Red Rock Park, had been ridiculed by the press. Uniformed federal marshals showed up at the campaign's first celebrity-laden fund-raising event at the Palace Theater in Los Angeles to confiscate money claimed by creditors from his first presidential campaign in 1984.

Hart had really been running for president since the moment after the roll call of the 1984 Democratic Convention in San Francisco, where former vice president Walter Mondale had secured the nomination after a hard-fought primary season. Mondale, a progressive Minnesota Democrat and former vice president during Jimmy Carter's administration, was widely and accurately seen as doomed to lose to Reagan. Hart would spend the fall campaigning for him, but the outcome was considered a foregone conclusion.

Ever since Mondale's decisive defeat in November, Hart was seen as the Democrats' presumptive 1988 nominee. When his second term in the Senate expired at the end of 1986 he kept his town house near the Capitol but moved his permanent residence back to Colorado and began to lay the groundwork for the 1988 campaign. Bonnie and I sold the first home we'd ever owned and moved from Washington to Colorado to join him. It meant leaving family, friends, jobs, and security, but there was a sense of adventure in the Rocky Mountain air, a sense of mission, a naive confidence, and nothing could have kept us away.

Hart had spent most of 1985 through early 1987 traveling to recruit campaign organizers, raise funds, and give speeches, all aimed at redefining and rebuilding a new Democratic Party. I accompanied him the entire way, editing speeches, handling local press and logistics, keeping him on schedule with the heel of my palm gently nudging into the small of his back, and capturing the names of new supporters we'd want to make part of the next campaign. I lived the campaign in the backseat, behind stage, doing in one hundred cities what my father had done for Congressman Moorhead in Pittsburgh: talking with supporters Hart couldn't spend enough time with, politely steering away the eccentrics and cranks after their quick photo or handshake, looking for trouble on the radar screen, and making sure it didn't enter Hart's airspace.

Of all the potential candidates, Hart had the best base of financial supporters, the strongest political network, and the best organization in the early battleground states of Iowa and New Hampshire. He also had the experience of having run once before. In contrast to 1984's underfinanced, dark-horse insurgency, the 1988 campaign—headquartered on his Colorado home turf and staffed by a young and energetic cadre of talented political organizers who knew each other well and worked smoothly together—was expected to be a professional, well-oiled machine. He was forty-nine years young, tested, and determined. His 1984 crusade had brought "a new generation of leadership" to the cusp of political power. That generation had tasted the possibility and promise of leadership and was poised to seize it.

Most important, the intellectual spadework of developing and honing a message with both substance and political appeal had been completed. Over the course of twelve years in the Senate he'd put together a team of economic policy advisers, arms control experts, farmers, teachers, and young leaders overseas who helped form and shape his views. Through speeches and articles Hart had not only put forth ideas on economic policy, foreign policy, education reform, and military strategy, but tried to tie them together in a unified, coherent way. He'd written two comprehensive policy books, *A New Democracy* and *America Can Win,* both serious, neither popular. "Prepared to govern. No on-the-job-training necessary," was the campaign mantra political director Paul Tully repeated to reporters over and over again.

Hart's senior staff and those closest to him knew any road to the White House was paved with enough land mines to make winning a long shot under the best of circumstances. Still, there was a sense that this time, it was ours to lose. Hart was equally confident of the gamble. He'd declined to run for a third term in the Senate to devote 100 percent of his energies to the presidential bid.

Though he often called several times a day, I was surprised to hear from him that Saturday evening. When he called, it was usually in the late morning, to see if there was anything he'd missed in the morning papers, any breaking news or important messages. His voice usually sounded deep, but distant, as if he were distracted, or perhaps reading a newspaper or editing a speech while we were talking. This night his voice was high and hesitant with a nervous laugh.

He told me he had some friends over, a man and two women, and that reporters from the *Miami Herald* were staking out his yard. He said I should call our campaign manager, Bill

Dixon, and that we should do something, but he didn't say what. It was a short phone call and he sounded preoccupied, as if he were trying to conduct more than one conversation at a time. Hart often called me to resolve minor problems. I assumed that was all this was. I felt confused but not alarmed.

I tried to reach Dixon at his apartment in downtown Denver, but his line was busy. I had fifty pages left to the novel I'd been reading so I put down the phone and picked up the book. The phone rang again minutes later. This time Hart sounded more disturbed. The reporters were still there, asking questions and taking pictures of him whenever he ventured outside his front door.

The next morning the *New York Times* made a front-page story of the *Miami Herald*'s investigation into Hart's personal life. Most of the nation's other leading papers followed suit. Ironically, the *New York Times Magazine* published a cover story on Hart that had been in the works for months that same Sunday. It concluded with Hart insisting his private life was boring and challenging the press, if they didn't believe him, to "follow me." This quote would be so widely reprinted in the following weeks that everyone thinks of it as the invitation that justified the *Miami Herald* reporters' staking out his house, though in fact its first publication came a day after they'd taken such liberties.

If Hart had been run over by the *Miami Herald* delivery truck the day before *Miami Herald* reporters staked out his front yard, the nation's leading papers—including the *Herald*—would have run front-page obituaries honoring a patriotic reformer who had inspired millions of people, particularly young people, to get involved in politics. He was an innovative and accomplished legislator, breaking new ground on issues of military reform, energy independence, and environmental quality, just to name a few. Does this excuse the way Hart and those of us on his staff handled the events that led to his withdrawal? Of course not.

Having come of age politically during the post-Watergate era, I had always hoped that if faced with a serious political crisis I might be the one person in the room with the presence of mind to speak truth to power, insist on confronting the cold, hard facts, and remind one and all that the truth always comes out in the end anyway. But that's not what I did. The campaign did not get all of the facts out in a straightforward manner, but rather got caught up in a web of inconsistencies that quickly undermined our credibility.

We spent days and nights on the lam trying to outwit our press pursuers with tactics like decoy motorcades, safe houses, and scheduling misinformation. Our trail ran from D.C. through New York to New Hampshire, where a frenzied press corps and family considerations finally persuaded Hart to call it quits and return home to Colorado.

That night my father called from Pittsburgh to console me and offer support, but the breaking of his voice as he choked back tears pained me and we kept the conversation short. We'd practiced our politics looking through opposite ends of the political telescope, giving me an expansive and breathtaking view of the whole nation, giving him an intimate, close-up look at one person at a time. What a gift it would be to be able to keep both in focus.

❧

Nearly a decade later, it's still difficult to place what happened in any kind of perspective. The reactions to Hart's transgressions and misjudgment were thermonuclear in scale, and he remains in a category all his own. Like his onetime colleague, former astronaut John Glenn, who was first to orbit the earth, there were others who followed whose exploits outshone his, but he was first and is the one we cannot forget.

I've spent much of the intervening years being asked, "What really happened that weekend?" or "Why did he do it?" or "How could he risk everything the way he did?" But as close as Hart and I were, we never discussed it then or since, and I never felt the need to. Perhaps this points to shortcomings of my own. It disappointed friends then and still does now.

The other question always asked is whether I felt angry or betrayed. And while I felt crushing disappointment, I was not angry with Gary Hart. Maybe because I loved and respected him and was willing to err on the side of always giving him the benefit of the doubt. And though my motives may have been less noble, I prefer to think it was because my principal fealty was to the ideas he proposed and stood for more than to the man himself, and for me they remain shining and untarnished.

Hart never suffered from a lack of confidence in his own ideas, and of at least one thing he was not only confident but certain: the awesome, waiting-to-be-tapped genuinely revolutionary power of youth. The first question he asked about every political contact I ever met was, "How old are they?" If he gambled anything in his career, it was that the energy, idealism, and commitment of inexperienced twenty-three-year-olds could triumph over the money, reputation, and conventional wisdom of their elders. That and the capacity of a relatively small number of young people to change or make history. He believed that passion and commitment won out over numbers every time. When he sent me on that first scouting trip to New Hampshire in June 1982, he cautioned, "Remember, the election is two years away. Our audience is not New Hampshire's voters or even New Hampshire's Democrats. We're campaigning for fifty people, maybe twenty-five. If we get the right twenty-five people at the core of our team, they'll get the next hundred twenty-five, and they'll get the next thousand. Politics is a series of concentric circles, and the most important circle is the first."

The lessons I learned from Hart will, I suspect, last a lifetime. They were lessons about seriousness of purpose, about the value of challenging basic premises and assumptions, about the resistance of entrenched interests to fundamental, institutional reform.

But when it was all over, I felt my last, best chance for public service through politics was over, too. I had been preparing for ten years for a role that no longer existed for me. My disappointment was not that I had worked so hard and come up short, but rather that I had learned so much that I'd have no opportunity to put to use. In time I would see that did not have to be the case.

There were the lessons about organizing that my sister, Debbie Shore, and I put to use in starting Share Our Strength and continue to use now: The theory of concentric circles that begins with an effort to organize just the handful of opinion-makers at its nucleus. The wisdom and necessity of decentralized operations that rely heavily on the advice and decisions of people on the ground who know their communities and their neighbors and know what they want and need. How to inspire people by recognizing their intelligence and talking up to them instead of condescending.

But above all else, there were the lessons about the power of ideas, the awesome, irresistible seduction of engaging people's hearts and minds and souls. The power that ideas have to move people, to motivate them, to sweep them up on behalf of a cause that is larger than their own personal interests and needs. The power that will lead them to willingly sacrifice hard-earned money, time with family, the selfish pleasures we all strive to deserve and earn. Hart saw ideas as the force that shaped the tides of history, the ammunition of battle, the fuel of revolutions.

4

*It seems to me that our three basic needs, for food and security
and love, are so mixed and mingled and entwined that we
cannot straightly think of one without the others. So it happens
that when I write of hunger, I am really writing about love and
the hunger for it, and warmth and the love of it and the hunger
for it . . . and then the warmth and richness and fine reality of
hunger satisfied . . . and it is all one. There is a communion of
more than our bodies when bread is broken and wine drunk.
And that is my answer when people ask me: Why do you write
about hunger, and not wars or love?*

M.F.K. FISHER

On a hot and lazy August morning in 1984 I was skimming the paper as I battled traffic on Interstate 270 on the way to work at Senator Hart's office. A brief article in the *Washington Post* carried the headline "200,000 to Die This Summer in Ethiopia." I'd had no previous knowledge of this tragedy in the making and was stunned by its enormity and the matter-of-fact nature of the reporting. The article ran somewhere on the bottom half of the front page. There was no follow-up story the next day. No analysis or editorial, either. Hart's 1984 presidential bid had come to an end at the convention in San Francisco less than thirty days earlier. We'd both taken brief vacations and were easing back into Senate life. It was a relaxed time that provided the opportunity to read parts of the paper I hadn't read in months, even if Interstate 270 wasn't the safest place for doing so.

I can't say I read the Ethiopian famine story and a light bulb went on. I'd never been to Ethiopia or shown much interest in it. But the story nagged at me. The potential loss of life was staggering. Four times the number of Americans who died in Vietnam. Every day's news includes its share of disasters, whether small or large, natural or man made, but this one seemed so preventable. The tragedy had not yet struck but the experts could see it coming. They could also see that nothing was going to be done to stop it. I was amazed that the world could remain oblivious to a catastrophe so imminent. I kept coming back to the story as I flipped through other sections of the paper. I wanted to do something about it. Not write a speech for someone else to deliver in the empty chamber of the Senate, or draft a letter for my senator to sign. I'd had plenty of experience with that already. I wanted to do something I could feel, something that would connect me with the people over there, touch their lives. I wasn't sure what it could be but all that day I thought about it and about who I might get to help. To me the newspaper story read like an invitation to act.

The experts were right. In the months that followed, famine arrived. Its devastation eventually became well established in the public consciousness, particularly with the broadcast of graphic film footage of starving, skeletal children. Eventually the world responded and tried to relieve what it did not prevent. But as of August, the *Washington Post* article was the first and only mention I'd seen. Having read it while decompressing from the exhausting grind of the 1984 campaign gave it added significance. We had spent months traveling to three or four states a day. Politics came before everything else. Friends, family, world events had been put on hold. And we were already thinking about the *next* campaign. The only part of the news we paid careful attention to were the political skirmishes that might affect the campaign's standing.

After reading about the starvation in more detail I had two reactions. One was a sense of shock and surprise that it wasn't treated as a more important story earlier.

The more arresting revelation, however, was that I felt anything at all. As I sat thinking about what the famine meant, what it must be like for the ravaged families who lived there, and what could be done, my feelings were less those of outrage than of simple gratitude that for the first time in years I had a reflex and opinion of my own. For the first time I really felt something about world events, made an emotional connection to them, beyond the usual calculations of how they could be turned to political advantage. On the staff of a presidential candidate you tend to develop and take on the views, ideologies, and reflexes of the candidate for whom you work. If not trained to do so, you are at least so conditioned.

Paul Tillich once wrote: "The stream of daily news, the waves of daily propaganda, and the tides of convention and sensationalism keep our minds occupied. The noise of these shallow waters prevents us from listening to the sounds out of the depth, to the sounds of what really happens in the ground of our social structure, in the longing hearts of the masses, and in the struggling minds of those who are sensitive to historical changes. Our ears are as deaf to the cries out of the social depth as they are to the cries out of the depth of our souls."

It had been at least three years since my ears had heard anything, since my soul had been touched, since I'd simply had an opinion of my own about anything. Now that I'd stumbled across one, I liked the feeling it gave me. Like a stray cat I'd meant to take in only for a moment, I was now reluctant to part with it. As the day went on I felt a stronger and stronger urge to commit myself personally to do something to help fight the hunger that was going to kill hundreds of thousands of people. Even if my contribution could be only a small one, it would be mine.

The idea of people going hungry has always struck me as one of exceptional poignancy. The need to eat not only unites us all but underscores a basic human frailty. Nature marks time in eons, yet each of us needs to eat every few hours, a fraction of time almost too infinitesimal for nature to measure. But the need is true and unrelenting for each and every one of us, no matter how rich or poor, powerful or oppressed, weak or strong—it is an emblem of our humanity. It's almost as if nature had created an infallible way to remind us, daily, regularly, that we are bound to and dependent upon every other living thing on the planet.

The antiwar marches on Washington, Robert Kennedy's fact-finding trips on poverty in Mississippi in the late 1960s, and Senator George McGovern's Senate hearings on hunger in

America helped to sharpen my generation's focus on America's priorities, and for this reason hunger had always exerted a powerful pull on my imagination. Whether in our own backyard or halfway around the world, hunger is the most basic and universal indicator of economic distress. Wherever you find people suffering from hunger, you find people without adequate health care, education, and economic opportunity.

One of my own household's occasional Saturday-morning rituals is to open the door of the kitchen pantry and have my nine-year-old son Zach and six-year-old daughter Mollie stand straight and tall with their backs against it while Mom and Dad place a grease pencil on top of their heads to measure and mark how much they've grown since the date of their last measurement. Anyone who has ever done this can attest to the sheer joy, pride, and self-esteem that children take away from their recognition of this simple and most natural of all acts: the act of growing.

But because of hunger, there are children in America not growing as they should be. They are underheight, underweight, and often neurologically and developmentally delayed and impaired. There is literally less to them than there should be. Physicians at urban hospitals treating children diagnosed as failing to thrive measure the circumferences of children's heads to track and chart the effects of malnutrition. Their research statistics confirm what doctors, teachers, and social workers see with their own eyes: too many children are hungry, malnourished, and failing to develop physically and mentally in ways necessary for their health and education.

Of everyone who is hungry in America, children are most vulnerable and have most at risk. A child's organs don't all grow at the same time. Each organ undergoes its own specific period for growth. If a nutritional deficiency occurs when a certain organ needs to be growing—like the brain, for example—the damage can be incalculable and irreversible. "The brain is like a unionized construction site," Boston City Hospital's Dr. Debra Frank once told Congress. "If you don't deliver the bricks when the crew is on the site, then the building is not going to be built normally."

At birth the brain is approximately 60 percent developed. At six months it has grown to 90 percent of its full size. The remaining growth takes place between six and eighteen months. After that the brain is fully grown. If it is not, well, too bad. Nothing can be done after eighteen months to cause brain tissue cells to further divide to make up for lost brain growth. The cells already there will expand and grow, but there will never be more of them, never as many as in the brain of a child whose nutritional requirements were satisfied. The short period of time at the very beginning of a child's life represents a large opportunity. Put the necessary resources into the right time and place at the start, and the healthy bodies and minds that result will reduce costs and pay dividends for a lifetime.

The most common nutritional problem seen in the United States today is anemia due to iron depletion. Iron sits at the center of a red blood cell. It is what the oxygen attaches itself to. Less iron means less oxygen circulating to the body's organs, in effect suffocating them. Anemic children weigh less and are shorter. They also have shorter attention spans, less ability to concentrate, and less curiosity. They are more susceptible to infectious disease. There are communities in urban areas of the United States where nearly the entire population is anemic by medical standards. But since hunger in America, thankfully, is not at the level where children starve and die in the streets, as was the case in Ethiopia and other developing countries, it is often hidden, disguised, denied, or ignored.

The challenge of fighting hunger here at home is compounded by enormous confusion and misunderstanding about who is hungry in America and why. The most common assumption is that hunger is confined to the many homeless people living on the streets or in the parks, or panhandling for spare change at subway stops. In fact the homeless people we see on the street are only a fraction of who is hungry in this country, and a misleading fraction at that. Not only do they not accurately represent the hungry in America, they don't even accurately represent who is homeless. Often mentally disturbed or alcohol or drug addicted, street people represent a fringe population and often have alternatives to the street that for one reason or another they have deemed unacceptable. These street people we pass on our way to work are poverty's dark shadow more than they are poverty itself. But they are the visible tip of a large iceberg. Submerged below the surface, less visible, are millions of Americans, most with homes and many with jobs, who are hungry each month.

In the early 1990s, for the first time in American history, 29 million Americans were on food stamps, more than 10 percent of the entire population. Almost none of them were homeless. The transient nature of homelessness makes it difficult, if not impossible, to receive food stamps. Almost one-third of the people using emergency food assistance have someone in their household who is employed, and almost half of those who are employed work full-time. In addition to food stamps, millions of

Americans require government-supported school lunch and breakfast programs, private assistance from food banks and soup kitchens, and other forms of emergency supplemental feeding. Nearly 43 percent of those using the nation's largest emergency assistance network, Second Harvest, are under the age of seventeen—a total of more than 10 million children.

America's wealth and bounty of food resources make hunger seem incongruous here. Our agricultural exports feed much of the world. Just the amount of food wasted every day could more than adequately feed Americans who are hungry. The fact that there is more than enough food for every man, woman, and child makes it seem as if the problem of hunger would be simple to solve. But this is probably the single most widely misunderstood aspect of hunger in America and what needs to be done about it.

It takes more than food to fight hunger. Using food to fight hunger is like using water to fight fire. On the surface it seems logical. But water is only the second best way to fight fire. Prevention is the first. Fire once destroyed entire cities and took thousands more lives than it does today. Better access to adequate water supplies, building codes, safety procedures, and stronger materials that make structures less susceptible to fire in the first place have made widespread urban fire catastrophes far less probable. In the case of hunger, like fire, prevention is the ultimate remedy.

But because emergency feeding assistance is simpler and more visible than the complex changes that would help ensure that fewer people need assistance in the first place, thousands of Americans donate food and volunteer in soup kitchens, but few dedicate themselves to activities that would help prevent hunger. More than 150,000 private organizations, relying heavily on volunteers, now pass out $3 billion to $4 billion worth of food annually. Few such organizations existed as recently as 1980. Their rapid growth is evidence that people in the United States do not want to let others go hungry. David Beckman, the President of the Bread for the World Institute, argues that "some of the effort devoted to helping hungry people should be directed toward transforming the politics of hunger." Noting that millions of people in the United States work through tens of thousands of organizations to help hungry people, he poses a provocative question: "Could this massive movement be transformed into a dynamic social and political movement with enough clout to end U.S. hunger and reduce world hunger?"

People who are hungry can't wait for the politicians to solve our economic and social problems. They need to eat now. But unless long-term efforts to prevent hunger are undertaken, the number of hungry Americans will continue to rise. Accordingly, any meaningful anti-hunger effort must recognize that hunger is only a symptom of the deeper problem of poverty.

Consider five-year-old Fidel from El Salvador whom Share Our Strength helped through a Failure to Thrive program at a maternal and child health clinic in Washington, D.C. His parents, practically illiterate, both work ten hours a day. Their combined annual salary of $12,000 is barely enough to bring food to the table for their family of five. Though an alert and intelligent child, Fidel was not growing. The clinic's nutritionist found he was below normal weight, height, and weight for height, reflecting his inadequate intake of food—he consumed no milk, no meat, and only a limited number of vegetables.

Fidel's main sources of nutrition were fruits, fruit juice, cereal, tortillas, and rice.

Fidel's malnourishment reflects poverty, hardship, and his parents' lack of education about nutrition. The nutritionist at the clinic taught his parents how to stretch their meager income among food and other basic necessities such as rent, electricity, and child care. And she monitored Fidel's dietary plan to bring him up to the twenty-fifth weight percentile. The clinic's director explained that "with repeated educational reinforcement from our nutritionist, pediatrician, home visiting teams, and health educator, parents will continue to learn the importance of a sound diet to their child's growth and development. *Our philosophy is that the most effective and enduring way of helping children is through provision of support to the entire family.* If parents feel competent and effective as individuals and as parents, they will be better able to love, nurture, and instill confidence in their children."

Look at the number of people involved in the effort to ensure that Fidel simply grows strong and healthy, and that his parents are equipped to nurture and support him. The director's words give life to the old proverb that it takes a whole village to raise a child.

Hungry people in the United States and hungry people in Ethiopia are both hungry because they lack food, but the reasons they lack food are quite different. Hunger around the world, especially the massive famines that capture world attention, is caused by war, famine, drought. Those who live in poverty are the most susceptible victims. Those are not the reasons for hunger in the United States, which are derived from poverty.

Some of the problems that face American society today are

complex, chronic, and seemingly insoluble. Hunger is not one of them. We know precisely what must be done to guarantee the nutrition necessary for the body and mind of a young child to grow properly. And we have the resources to do it. We simply haven't had the will. We've got no shortage of food resources in the United States, only a shortage of leadership necessary to ensure the economic conditions that will give every American access to that food. As Dr. Larry Brown, director of the Tufts University Center on Hunger, Poverty and Nutrition, once told a group of Share Our Strength organizers: "Somehow, hunger in America is a metaphor for a nation that has lost course . . . a people whose best values are not being reflected in the policies of its government."

Though the story of the Ethiopian famine broke as I was moving back to Hart's Senate staff from his presidential campaign staff, it did not occur to me to suggest a legislative response for him to pursue, even though at one time this would have been an almost involuntary reflex. In the Senate you could read an article in the *Washington Post* in the morning, draft a legislative response by noon, and have your senator introduce it as a bill before the day was over. But often results were a long way off. The chain of events to achieve legislative satisfaction is long and laborious: drafting and introducing a bill, committee hearings and approval, votes in the House and Senate, then a conference committee to resolve differences, and finally the president signing the bill into law. After that, it is necessary to oversee the appropriate agencies to make sure they carry out the law. At any step along the way a good idea can be derailed. This process helps bad ideas get derailed as well, which was why the Founding Fathers structured our government as they did.

But it wasn't the slowness of the process that discouraged me. It was that instead of serving a purpose, the process had become the purpose. Given the slow pace of Capitol Hill, you might never see the beneficial results of your legislative victory. So you take satisfaction from more accessible landmarks along the way—whether your senator received favorable press coverage, whether an action improved his standing in the polls, his ability to raise money, or his chances for reelection. But these are not the reasons you went to work in politics in the first place. The victories are hollow, the stuff of scrapbooks. Whenever the chase takes on greater importance than what you're chasing after, it's time to look for another way.

So what occurred to me instead of legislation or government action, as necessary as both were, was to create a private organization that would act on the impulse to help—one that would specifically raise funds for the hunger relief efforts that were already in place and under way but underfunded. I had never started such an organization and didn't belong to any. A private organization, especially a new one, probably couldn't contribute more than a drop in a bucket, but at least it would be a start. And besides, even if its impact this time was small, at least it would be up and running, ready and stronger, for the next time, wherever and whenever it came.

When I thought about who in the United States might connect to issues of food and hunger, the restaurant and food service industry naturally came to mind. One of the largest industries in the United States, it has a presence in virtually every neighborhood, whether large or small, rich or poor. Everyone involved makes their livelihood from the basic fact of life that all people need food. And standing behind the chefs and restaurants are growers, suppliers, distributors, advertisers, and others that comprise a vast national network. Those who work in the industry see a tremendous amount of food go to waste. I was convinced they would be sympathetic.

Perhaps best of all, they were an untapped resource. One of the great needs in the fight against hunger, as in the effort to advance any social cause, is to expand the constituency of people who care about the issue beyond the professional advocates, legislative aides, politicians, and others who slip into the comfortable groove of fighting the same battles year after year, each time with slightly less energy and idealism than the time before, their vision of what is possible constrained and confined by the disappointing realities of the past. If the community of activists already involved in anti-hunger and anti-poverty efforts were enough by themselves to get the job done, then we wouldn't have the conditions that we have in the first place. My interest was in bringing new people and new dollars to the effort, in addition to new energy, excitement, and creativity. The goal was not to preach to the converted, but to convert more.

The last thing I wanted to do was to start yet another organization that spent a lot of money just to beg for more money through shrill direct-mail solicitations or guilt-inducing photos of starving babies. Depending on charitable donations is both unreliable and limiting. Leftover wealth is not a very sturdy foundation upon which to build a new vision. There were many groups already doing that. And it wasn't enough. We couldn't have the necessary impact on hunger by competing with other organizations for our slice of the charitable pie and then redistributing those dollars along the lines of our own vision. New and previously untapped dollars and resources needed to be brought into the effort. New wealth needed to be created.

To accomplish this required organizing creative individuals to fight hunger through their own unique skills, talents, and experience. Not by asking them for money, but by soliciting a more valuable gift, the gift of their special strengths. Chefs would be asked to cook or to teach cooking, writers to write or to read from their work, artists to create art. The organization would transform such gifts into the dollars needed to support community hunger organizations around the country.

When people contribute through their unique skills and creative abilities they are giving the one thing that is most genuinely theirs and that no one can take away. Their contribution need not be dependent upon their net worth, cash flow, or the approval of their employer. What they are giving is what is at their core, and once tapped, it unleashes lasting energy and commitment.

I also did not want to start something and not finish it. I wanted to develop a source of financial support that would be steady and reliable over time, not just a blip on the screen resulting from one high-profile event, like a concert or benefit, but a source of funding on which recipient agencies around the United States and around the world could come to rely.

Within a few months some very creative people would mount some ambitious campaigns that had an impact on hunger relief greater than anyone could have imagined. USA for Africa's all-star recording of "We Are the World" and the Hands Across America event that inspired tens of thousands of Americans to line up across the country and raise money for hunger relief both did an enormous amount of good, and their impact is still felt. But impressive as these projects were, they left no structure in place through which people could continue to contribute. When the events were over, they were over.

The goal was to build an organization at the place where public interest and private interest intersect. It seemed like the place most likely to sustain an effort over the long term. Those being asked for their help would also gain something in return. It would be in their self-interest and in their business interest to get involved. Our goal would be to build something, methodically and as slowly as need be, but aimed at leaving an institution for sustained and reliable funding in place.

The challenge was to create an organization that participants would feel was genuinely theirs, rather than an organization that would simply use them to help itself grow. They wouldn't just contribute to and support the organization—they would be it. Their energies would not be devoted to helping the organization grow; instead, its growth would be devoted to releasing their energies. We named it Share Our Strength.

❦

On November 8, 1984, I wrote Senator Hart a memo outlining my idea and seeking his indulgence for starting this new organization. It was an unusual and unconventional request. The effort would clearly require more than just my spare time. A senator needs, or at least expects, his staff to be at his beck and call twenty-four hours a day. Staff members are not expected to be distracted by any outside interests. But Hart was an unconventional politician and had developed a confidence in my instincts as I had in his. Without his support there was no way I could proceed.

For several days I waited anxiously for my memo to make

its way through the pipeline. Hart typically had dozens of staff memos, letters from Senate colleagues, press releases, and speech drafts awaiting his comment and approval. Ensuring that he review these in a timely and orderly fashion was a full-time job for his personal assistant. His response, written across the top of my memo in the blue felt pen that was his signature style, was enthusiastically positive. The first thing I did after renting an office space for SOS was to tack it on the wall above my desk. I didn't know at the time that his words of encouragement would be almost all any of us would have to keep us going during the frustrations and setbacks of the next twenty-four months.

Before Share Our Strength was an organization it was an idea. And before that, it was an emotion, a reflex, a response. I've always thought of the impulse that gave birth to SOS as my response to the horrors of the Ethiopian famine, but I can see now that it was a response to that and more. It was also a response to a decade's toil in the trenches of congressional policy making— the triumphs and the disappointments, a response to the superficiality of presidential politics, a response to a childhood made comfortable by caring and compassionate parents. It was the turning of a corner from a place where I'd always seen government or business or some other institution as having the principal responsibility for solving social problems to a place where I'd come to see the responsibility, and the promise, that I and others like me held.

When acclaimed concert pianist Richard Goode was asked what advice he had for young musicians he explained: "Pay attention to your deepest response to the music, get as close to it as possible. I don't think there is an external path to something like that. Your strength as a performer comes from where your need is—from saying the things in music you really have to say. Audiences will respond to that—they hear the accent of honest feeling."

The single most essential ingredient in converting a response into the founding of an organization, a company, a building, or a movement is that it be built from a vision that is uniquely yours. If your vision is based on a deep-seated need of your own, you will not fail. Your need will not let you. Whether you need to do something about education, juvenile justice, clean air, domestic violence, or whether you need to paint a landscape, build a house, or start a business, your strength will come from where your need is, as surely as a baby's strength comes from the need for its mother's milk. And as Richard Goode noted, you will be more convincing in communicating that vision, more persuasive than anyone else could ever be, more persuasive than you could be about any other idea, because people will hear and be convinced by "the accent of honest feeling."

❦

Share Our Strength crossed the threshold from idea to reality when my sister, Debbie Shore, and I rented a one-room basement office in a house on Capitol Hill, three blocks from the Senate office buildings. We found a lawyer to file articles of incorporation with the federal government, draft bylaws, and get 501(c)(3) status from the IRS so that contributions to SOS would be tax deductible. We borrowed a typewriter and with some stencils from the five-and-dime made stationery.

I called Steve Wozniak, the inventor of the Apple Computer, whom I had once met to ask if he would donate a computer. He did more. He told me he had actually left Apple but still had privileges in the company store. "I'll just go over and buy a few of them, and a daisy wheel printer, and put them on a plane," he said. "I better send my assistant along to train you, too."

The initial concept was simple and naive. Restaurants who contributed to Share Our Strength would get a *Good Housekeeping*–type seal of approval with the SOS logo to display prominently while SOS found ways to promote the logo that would increase their business. Five percent of the 450,000 restaurants in the United States contributing $500 a year would yield more than $11 million a year, which sounded like a large sum of money at that time. The math was accurate. But the reasoning was flawed.

With Steve Wozniak's computer we compiled lists and mailed letters to chefs, restaurant owners, hotels, franchisees. Thousands of letters. Then we waited. And waited. And waited. A few true believers sent money. Mostly there was silence. Each day we eagerly waited for the mail but it never seemed to come. Our basement-level office had a window near the ceiling that put the mailman's ankles at eye level. I got to know those ankles well as I watched them pass us by day after day without even slowing. Once there were more than twenty-five days straight with no mail. I literally ran up the concrete steps and followed the mailman down the street, at first inquiring politely, hesitantly, about where our mail might be, then, the next day, driven to the edge by desperation, demanding that a trace be put on the mail I was convinced was missing.

A breakthrough came when Alice Waters, a widely admired innovator of American cooking in Berkeley, California, sent a check for $1,000 and asked how else she could help. Respected by restaurateurs and food writers across the country, she was the person we'd been waiting for. We used her support to reach a small handful of opinion makers in the restaurant community who would be impressed and influenced by her support. Nearly $20,000 came in response to her letter. Whenever another prominent chef came on board we'd ask him or her to do the same. It was the theory of concentric circles that Hart had used in New Hampshire in 1984. Within weeks, a dozen of the nation's best-known chefs were acting as our ambassadors to their colleagues.

The early money raised was like picking the low-hanging fruit. Very soon the effort got tougher; no one gets turned on by dropping a check in the mail. For two years we struggled, chased mailmen, missed payroll, and reread encouraging comments tacked up on the wall.

When my family moved to Denver at the end of 1986 for Hart's second presidential run, SOS moved there as well. The leaders of Denver's restaurant community mounted the first food-and-wine benefit that served as the model for the series of grassroots events that became "Taste of the Nation."

We learned it was easier to get chefs to spend $500 to $1,000 to cover the costs of participating in a hunger relief event than to get them to send as little as $100 through the mail once a year. Why? Because they preferred to contribute through their skills and feel more connected to the cause. They took pride in being united with their colleagues across the nation. The visibility at a large public event and the chance to meet potential customers was good for business, too. We wanted it to be in their interest to continue their participation.

After the successful Denver event we decided to hold such

events all across the country at around the same time. From a yacht that circles the Statue of Liberty in New York to the Cowboy Hall of Fame in Oklahoma, dozens of each city's best chefs would gather to serve a specialty item or signature dish. They were joined by distributors pouring as many as fifty different wines. Because of the prominence of the chefs and restaurateurs involved, as well as the demographics of the patrons—upscale diners who patronize restaurants—cognac companies, bottled water distributors, national coffee brands, and others paid sponsorship fees for the exclusive right to serve their products. These sponsorship fees enabled SOS to distribute 100 percent of the ticket proceeds of such events to community-based anti-hunger efforts. Nothing was taken out for costs or administrative expenses, which gave SOS a competitive advantage over other fund-raising events.

In "Taste of the Nation"'s first full year—1988—events were held in eighteen cities and a total of $252,000 was raised. In 1989, it more than doubled, to $680,000, and again the next year to $1.2 million. By 1995 the events were netting more than $4.3 million.

The money was crucial but so was the awareness that was raised. Tens of thousands of people got information and literature about hunger-relief efforts in their own community. In Portsmouth, New Hampshire, for example, the local paper, the *Portsmouth Herald,* ran a headline before our 1994 event proclaiming "Hunger Benefit Triples Goal," and quoted the chief executive of the Portsmouth-based Newmarket Software Systems, the local sponsor, saying: "Hunger is a problem right here in our own backyard. In order to make a difference we must make fundamental changes in the way we think about hunger."

REVOLUTION *of the* HEART

People expect to see politicians and anti-hunger activists quoted in their newspapers about social issues, but creating an opportunity for business leaders to talk about hunger brings credible new voices to the public dialogue, helping to expand the constituency of people who care about the cuase.

Except for a paid staff in Washington, our national "Taste" network is all volunteer. Decentralized by necessity, the chefs involved not only participate in the event, they create and organize it, calling on others in their industry, including accountants, public relations consultants, and restaurant critics.

The lessons learned from soliciting non-monetary contributions were reinforced when, by coincidence, unsolicited checks came in the mail from two best-selling writers: Stephen King and Sidney Sheldon. It presented an opportunity to ask writers to write more than checks. We asked them to contribute by writing stories. The result was an anthology called *Louder Than Words,* published by Random House's Vintage Books, to which twenty-two top writers contributed new work. Our contract with the publisher was a standard one, except that SOS, and not a writer, would be paid royalties from the book's sales.

One of the anthology's contributors was Anne Tyler, the Pulitzer Prize–winning novelist. Tyler wrote a story, which we sold to *Ladies' Home Journal* for $3,500. If I had asked for $3,500 over the phone it would not have been a very long conversation, yet she loved the idea of donating a story. A check would have taken less than a minute to write. The story took weeks. But the contribution made her feel more connected to our work. Another contributing author, Michael Downing, explained: "I thank you for the privilege of giving away something of value. I typically find myself writing rather inconsequential checks, which I try to inflate with goodwill and best wishes. It is a joy to know that my contribution's value will appreciate because of your work and the contributions of others."

Louder Than Words led to several more collections, a series of children's books, and a cookbook, and spawned other innovative ideas. Novelist Fred Busch raised a few hundred dollars at a local reading and sent the money with the suggestion the idea be replicated and expanded into a national event: writers across the country would read from their work one night of the year. The result was Writers Harvest, in which more than eight hundred writers read in nearly two hundred cities, all on the same night, charging for admission and enabling SOS to donate 100 percent of the proceeds to local anti-hunger efforts. "The words we writers speak at the Writers Harvest readings become, through our contribution, the bread of life for the hungry and the disadvantaged all across the country," author Charles Baxter said. "We are fortunate to have an opportunity to use our gifts this way."

Share Our Strength's continued growth is due to many creative and compassionate individuals who seized it as their own, bringing a diverse mix of energy and ideas that continue to replenish and strengthen the organization. Father Brian Frawley, who served as a parish priest in the Bronx for eight years before joining the SOS staff, once observed that SOS's values "seem to touch others in such a way that they are mystified and attracted, not to us, but to what we believe about them and the unrealized possibilities that they possess within."

The results speak for themselves. SOS now has over 100,000 contributors. A groundbreaking partnership with American

Express has more than doubled the size of the organization and helped build other partnerships with Northwest Airlines, Universal Studios, Seagram's, Fetzer Vineyards, Barnes and Noble, Starbucks Coffee, Calphalon Cookware, Gallo Wines, and many more. In 1996 Share Our Strength will raise and spend more than $16 million to support community-based efforts aimed at both relieving and preventing hunger. None of this money comes from the government, nor will it come from other foundations or direct mail. Instead, new wealth will be generated and new dollars will be brought to the effort so that all groups fighting hunger and poverty can benefit.

5

History says, Don't hope
On this side of the grave.
But then, once in a lifetime
The longed-for tidal wave
Of justice can rise up
And hope and history rhyme.

So hope for a great sea-change
On the far side of revenge.
Believe that a further shore
Is reachable from here.
Believe in miracles
And cures and healing wells.

SEAMUS HEANEY
The Cure at Troy

America needs a new public philosophy. The poverty destroying a generation of children, combined with the persistent failure of social policy, billions of wasted tax dollars, and the increasing irrelevance of both political parties demands it. Ten years' experience building a unique organization suggests one: sharing strength.

If this philosophy of building community by sharing one's strength instead of relying solely on government or the market-

75

place sounds idealistic, it is idealism without illusions. It is built upon a two-part strategy both practical and proven, a strategy fundamentally rooted in the success of American free enterprise.

The first component of the strategy is strengthening community by strengthening the institutions through which we build community. Community-based nonprofit organizations must be reconceived and reinvented so they not only redistribute wealth, but actively create the new wealth necessary to meet future needs. The second component is supplementing that wealth with a new community currency comprised of our own hands-on efforts. Taken together, these new concepts will give communities the money, resources, and tools they need to support children, make neighborhoods safer, provide services to those in need, and help more people get to the point where they can support themselves.

This strategy does not require a new law, government agency, appropriation, or tax credit. All it requires is a new way of thinking about our responsibility as citizens and a willingness to learn the language of community.

Every day millions of Americans wage an uphill battle to improve their lives and the quality of life in their community. They serve meals at soup kitchens, volunteer at AIDS clinics, increase awareness of domestic violence, read to children after school or on weekends, build playgrounds in the inner city, help clean a river or wilderness area, and seek to serve in countless other ways. But anyone who has done so knows how frustrating it can be when the organization for which you volunteer is short of the necessary resources, lacks skilled staff, and is not as organized as it should be. The overwhelming majority of the 570,000 community nonprofit institutions in the United States are underfinanced and overworked, constantly preoccupied by fund-raising needs, and unable to perform on a scale equal to the need they seek to address. This undermines citizen participation and virtually forfeits the task of community building to government agencies poorly equipped to handle it.

Citizens can best share their strengths and meaningfully participate in community through strong community institutions. We lack them. There are many reasons why but the most important are financial. Put simply, community nonprofit institutions are weak because they do not have the money they need to do their job. Stiff competition for charitable dollars and cuts in government funding are partly responsible. But the nonprofits themselves bear responsibility as well.

The nonprofit sector of society is rich in compassion and idealism, but it is entrepreneurially bankrupt, stuck in the posture of settling for that tiny margin of the financial universe that consists of leftover wealth—the excess funds people are willing and able to donate after their other primary needs have been met. Depending on leftover wealth to fight poverty is like trying to get a tractor trailer to the top of a hill by depending upon passersby to push it in their spare time rather than creating a powerful engine that will take it there. Of all the ways in a free society to amass the resources necessary to do great and important things, relying on other individuals or institutions to give away whatever portion of their own money they've concluded they may not need seems like the most lame. I call it the "Blanche Dubois Syndrome" because, like the character in *A Streetcar Named Desire,* nonprofits find themselves at the mercy of the kindness of strangers.

Too many nonprofit organizations are financially stagnant, raising and distributing funds the same way they have for decades. An extraordinary amount of time is devoted to finding new methods of soliciting charitable contributions through events such as benefit dinners, fashion shows, golf tournaments, walkathons, 10-K runs, "gold circle" memberships for large donors, and movie premieres. Such ideas are increasingly clever and make contributing enjoyable for donors. But they expand across only a finite universe of charitable dollars. Total charitable giving in the United States amounts to $130 billion a year, but less than $12 billion of that is aimed at human services for the poor. The highest levels of giving often go to museums, symphonies, private colleges, and the like—institutions whose patrons partake of their services. Even if the best charitable intentions were combined and doubled, it would not be enough to pay for the work that needs to be done on behalf of our children, families, and neighborhoods.

Most nonprofits are also heavily dependent on government money. Catholic Charities, one of the nation's largest, is a network of more than 1,400 agencies across the United States that in 1993 received over $1.25 billion in federal, state, and local funds. More than 40 percent of funding for United Way agencies comes from contracts with government. The Salvation Army receives about 17 percent of its revenue from government, but in some areas the figure is as high as 86 percent. Government agencies will give more than $5 billion to major nonprofits this year. According to *U.S. News and World Report,* "Nationally, charities now get about 30 percent of their funding from government, and many programs get more than half their money from government. Some, such as nursing homes and orphanages, can rely on government for at least 75 percent of their funding." This doesn't make these organizations bad. Indeed, since the 1960s private charities have become one of the government's preferred service providers because of the efficiency and compassion with which they are able to do their job. But it does put them in the position of redistributing wealth, not creating it.

Government funds, charitable solicitations, and foundation grants all have one thing in common: they represent somebody else's money. Nonprofits that rely on these sources shift limited dollars from one place to another, dividing the philanthropic pie rather than taking steps to create a bigger pie. For the last half of the twentieth century the Achilles' heel of traditional liberalism has been its penchant for redistributionist economic policies, its focus on providing resources for the "have-nots" by taxing those resources away from the "haves." Whether or not that approach was just, the result has been a conservative political backlash that won the political sympathy of the middle class and weakened support for the liberal social agenda. Voter rebellion has forced the political community to absorb that lesson. The philanthropic community has not yet done so and today finds itself in the same trap.

Redistributing leftover wealth is a narrow, perverse, and self-defeating posture that virtually dooms community non-profit organizations to fall short of fulfilling their missions. It is reactive. It is counterstrategic. It is shamefully wasteful. And it is profoundly ironic. An entire population of disadvantaged Americans are, because of welfare, viewed rightly or wrongly as an "underclass" surviving on and becoming dependent upon handouts that don't enable them to even meet their families' needs. So how do those who are their champions support their own efforts to create programs to help them? In most cases, *through handouts*—or at least a form of handouts also known as foundation or government grants.

These hard truths about nonprofits are often obscured or forgiven in light of the talented, good-hearted, and well-meaning people who labor within the nonprofit universe on behalf of the most righteous of causes. Those who have built careers in the nonprofit sector often undertake enormous challenges. Almost all have sacrificed financially. Some literally risk their lives. They are true heroes, community leaders, and neighbors in the best sense of the words. And while they do a world of good, it's not good enough. They not only deserve better but the scope of our problems demands it. The end result of the current situation is tragic: Nonprofits built upon bold and compassionate visions don't have the resources to fulfill their mission; staff burn out or are forced to leave because of financial strain; and vitally needed services go undelivered. If America's military institutions, health care providers, or banks had stagnated to the same degree over the last forty years, it would be seen as the national crisis that it is.

The reasons the nonprofit community continues along this path are clear but not compelling. First, it is simply the way things have always been done. Comfort is the enemy of change. An entire industry of nonprofit and philanthropic executives are comfortable doing things the way their predecessors did them. A multitude of seminars, conferences, newsletters, and nonprofit associations are devoted to passing along and reinforcing fund-raising techniques that reinforce the old methods.

Second, the nonprofit community is a decentralized and highly diverse community of predominantly local organizations without any type of national or coordinating leadership and without the vision that leadership could provide. Innovation is episodic and slow to take hold.

Third, too many nonprofits put themselves on a pedestal and take for granted that what they are doing is so important that people will financially support them just because the work is good and right. But in a competitive nonprofit marketplace those reasons may not be compelling enough, and even if they were, the charitable universe is not large enough to meet current needs.

Finally, social activists tend to have a healthy, but often excessive distrust of the business community. Indeed the massive accumulation of wealth and profit are often viewed with suspicion. They have few natural relationships with businesspeople, little business experience of their own, and few of the skills in sales, marketing, investing, or other financial strategies that are valuable and necessary for creating profit. As a result, strategies to generate wealth based on business practices are not a natural reflex.

Because nonprofits are so dependent on charity, they suffer from a related problem that goes to the heart of their inability to develop and execute more strategic agendas for success. The problem is that instead of determining the level of resources necessary to solve a certain problem, most nonprofits determine the level of resources they think is available to them from traditional charitable or governmental sources and set their goals accordingly. That's backward logic. By allowing fixed resources to determine the scope of their mission rather than fixing their mission and determining what resources are necessary to achieve it, failure becomes a self-fulfilling prophecy.

❦

None of this should be construed as an intent to dismiss the value and importance of charity, or to suggest that the pursuit of charitable support is bad or dishonorable. It is not. The sum total of charitable giving in this country has produced some fantastic results and reflects the best and most generous aspects of the American character. Every nonprofit institution ought to go out and get every private and public dollar available. But the point is that they should not limit themselves to philanthropic dollars if they can help it. There's nothing wrong with appealing to people's generosity and charitable instincts. But why stop there? Why not appeal to their self-interest as well? Self-interest is and always has been one of the most powerful profit generators. Why should the for-profit business world have that monopoly? Why not develop a business that produces products and services that people want and need and thereby generates profit and creates wealth? For nonprofit organizations to rely only on charitable, foundation, and government grants is working just one side of the street. And despite the generosity of donors, it is foolhardy to ignore the stores, industries, manufacturers, and services on the other side of the street.

The for-profit sector of society embodies a completely different mind-set and yields lessons that nonprofits have too long ignored. In the for-profit sector anyone who wants to build or create something—from movie studio executives to car manufacturers—must find ways to make their goals publicly appealing and profitable so that they can marshal the resources necessary to achieve them. When they make expenditures for things nobody wants to buy, they must subsidize those expenditures with revenues from products or services that people do want and pay for. Ford Motor Company doesn't have a showroom where customers can come in and buy research on next year's Taurus station wagon or health care for Ford Employees. Why would anyone pay for that? Instead Ford can afford to pay for it by building it into the cost of their products. Community-based nonprofits, virtually by definition, must pay for programs and services that otherwise lack their own constituency of paying customers. Like Ford Motor Company, they should consider using money generated by other goods and services to do so.

Increasingly there have been businesses, such as Ben and Jerry's Ice Cream, Anita Roddick's Body Shops, American Express, and Timberland, that explicitly earmark a percentage of profits to support public-interest activities. These progressive enterprises represent an important trend that began in the 1980s and brought entirely new resources to bear on behalf of community activities. Now the time has come to take this one step further, to turn the tables and do it the other way around. Instead of a business deciding what nonprofit causes to support with some of its excess profits, nonprofits need to decide what line of business they can devise to create the profits needed to support their public-interest efforts. To meet the challenges of the future, nonprofits must be thoroughly reinvented to create new wealth—that is, *nonprofits for profit.*

❦

A nonprofit that is run for profit sounds like a contradiction in terms. But it doesn't have to be. This new type of entrepreneurial hybrid is what I call a Community Wealth Enterprise.

A Community Wealth Enterprise creates wealth by providing a product or service of value, by selling something that people want to buy for reasons independent of their charitable intentions. But the wealth it generates is returned to the community in the form of direct services or grants to community-based service providers. Such organizations are relatively new and so rare as to be considered endangered species. But the few organizations that merit the label Community Wealth Enterprise (CWE) provide clear and convincing evidence that this is an idea whose time has come, one that is well suited to the political and social climate of the 1990s and beyond.

Community Wealth Enterprises have specific characteristics that distinguish them from traditional nonprofit organizations:

• A CWE does not simply redistribute inherited wealth or interest from an endowment or disburse government money. A CWE actively creates new wealth, as SOS has done by tapping into the creativity of writers, chefs, and artists, and by contracting with corporate partners to provide unique marketing opportunities. As a result, there is an opportunity to create vast new resources to support social change. There will always be large and powerful foundations established as the legacies of great family wealth like Ford or Rockefeller—foundations that are capitalized on "old money" and simply manage principal and spend interest along beneficent lines. They play a vital role in supporting the arts, human services, medical research, education, and more. Our society is fortunate for the generous impulses that underlie them and for the great work they do. But the new sources of funds will not be yielded by foundation investment but rather created by entrepreneurs who have turned their skills toward the public interest.

• A CWE creates that wealth by providing a product or service of value, by selling something that people want to buy for reasons that complement, but go above and beyond, their purely charitable intentions. These can range from simple food-and-wine festivals, to clothing and furniture, to complex marketing and promotional contracts with major corporations.

- CWE revenues are less dependent on trends in charitable giving but more dependent upon the wants and needs expressed through the free market. This means CWEs are not as vulnerable to what those in philanthropic circles call "compassion fatigue."

- Revenues that are generated by CWEs have no strings attached, which is often not the case with either government or foundation funding. This means that the organization can spend the money as it sees fit, in accordance with its best judgment, and not in ways distorted by the desire to please certain grant makers or support popular programs over less popular ones that might be more deserving. Unrestricted funds are the most valuable revenues for any organization.

- A CWE returns wealth directly back to the community in the form of vitally needed services such as teaching, training, or building, or through cash grants to other community-based service providers. Almost all nonprofits, from the zoo to the symphony, would argue that communities benefit from their work in "quality of life" terms, and they do. But in the case of CWEs these benefits are tangible, measurable resources that have been transferred to community-based service organizations.

- Because it is creating new wealth, a CWE does not directly compete with other nonprofits for scarce charitable dollars. Instead it brings potential new donors into the community from which all organizations can benefit. The end result is that instead of money simply being shifted from one pot to another, or more accurately, away from one charitable enterprise and toward another, the cumulative pot gets larger. Most nonprofits draw down the well of resources available for charitable or public interest activities. CWEs bring new water to the well, from which all can benefit. And since they are not competing directly—at least not in the traditional fashion—CWEs make cooperation among nonprofits more feasible, whereas in the past they have tried to work together but have often eyed each other warily.

Because they create new wealth, Community Wealth Enterprises increase commerce and add to the economy's growth, just as any for-profit business enterprise would. Goods and services are manufactured, marketed, distributed, and sold. Businesses expand and jobs are created or sustained as a result of this commerce. Government collects more taxes from a broader base. So in addition to having the direct effect of raising funds for social services, such organizations also enhance the general economic well-being of the community at large, if only to the same small extent as any one company would in the overall scheme of things.

It would be too idealistic, perhaps, to think that an appropriate wealth-generating or Community Wealth Enterprise activity could be found for each and every kind of charitable cause or social service. Many organizations, including those that protect and advocate for minority views or unpopular positions, may not enjoy the support necessary to create a wealth-generating financial base. There are many that will always have to rely on philanthropic dollars and charitable intentions. But where ingenuity and enterprise can bring other, additional resources to the table, it must.

In many ways it is astounding that the social service and nonprofit community has not yet embraced the creation of wealth as a means to serve its ends. Creating wealth is a simple and direct route to attaining the resources needed to do good things. It is proven and time tested. The for-profit community has been doing it for centuries. Though there are undeniably many in business only to make money, there are countless examples of visionary leaders who used their business and its profits to effect social change, not just by using profits for charitable purposes, but by using the profits to support a business that in and of itself leaves a positive impact on society in accordance with its own vision.

There's a long history of visionary companies building and using enormous financial resources to further specific ideologies that are about much more than just making money or increasing stock value. The leaders of Microsoft, for example, want to lead an information revolution. They may be getting rich in the process, but money is not their only goal. They never thought to finance their dreams through foundation grants, charitable solicitations, or direct-mail solicitations. They did not permit the realization of their dream to become dependent on whether someone else had leftover wealth to donate for their use. Rather they had to create something of value, something that people wanted to buy, to pay for the ingredients of what they wanted to build.

A fascinating new body of research has been brought to light by James Collins and Jerry Porras, professors at the Stanford University Business School and the authors of *Built to Last,* a study of the traits and habits of America's most successful companies and the practices and philosophies that made them so. Although the book was written for business entrepreneurs, nonprofit managers have much to learn from it. The book focuses on eighteen exceptional and long-lasting companies (Walt Disney, American Express, Merck, IBM, Sony, Johnson & Johnson, just to name a few) that have an average age of nearly one hundred years and have outperformed the general stock market by a factor of fifteen since 1926.

In a chapter titled "Exploding the Profit Myth" they describe one of their most intriguing findings: "Contrary to business school doctrine, we did not find 'maximizing shareholder wealth' or 'profit maximization' as the dominant driving force or primary objective through the history of most of the visionary companies." Instead, they concluded, "Profitability is a necessary condition for existence and a means to more important ends, but it is not the end in itself for many of the visionary companies. Profit is like oxygen, food, water, and blood for the body; they are not the point of life but without them, there is no life." This is not to say that visionary companies don't seek profits. They do. But the research demonstrates they are equally guided by a sense of ideology, values, and purpose beyond just money making. "Paradoxically, the visionary companies make more money than the more purely profit-driven comparison companies."

Their research describes the founding of Johnson & Johnson in 1886, when Robert W. Johnson stated his aim "to alleviate pain and disease." In the early 1900s one of J & J's researchers explained how this affected the research department: "The department is not conducted in any narrow, commercial spirit . . . and not kept going for the purpose of paying dividends or solely for the benefit of Johnson & Johnson, but with a view to aiding the progress of the art of healing." Their study also cites David Packard's explanation of Hewlett-Packard's operating philosophy: "You can look around and still see people who are interested in making money and nothing else, but the underlying drive comes largely from a desire to do something else—to make a product, to give a service—generally to do something which is of value. . . . Profit is not the proper end and aim of management—it is what makes all of the proper ends and aims possible."

It would be easy to be cynical about these public-spirited pronouncements, especially that of pharmaceutical founder George Merck, who claimed, "We try never to forget that medicine is for the people. It is not for the profits. The profits follow and if we have remembered that, they have never failed to appear. The better we have remembered it, the larger they have been." Indeed Collins and Porras readily acknowledge that the companies they studied could afford to have high ideals. But the whole point of their research is that idealism proved to be pragmatic because the more ideological the visionary company, the more highly effective a profit-making enterprise it turned out to be.

There are dozens of other examples, but the fundamental point is clear: Those who have set out to make great achievements in the business world have incorporated profit and the creation of wealth as a means toward that end. Though it has proved to be an effective strategy, it is all but ignored by the nonprofit world. Five days a week the *Wall Street Journal* documents the creation of wealth in this country and around the world in an infinite number of ways as well as the resulting unquantifiable financial resources. Why not use some of these ideas to create community wealth?

For the first time, this is beginning to happen through a new breed of public-service entrepreneurs who set out to make money through business—not for personal profit, but for the explicit and exclusive purpose of doing good. Here are a few examples of entrepreneurs building Community Wealth Enterprises:

• Citizens Energy is a nonprofit company that was established in 1979 by Joseph Kennedy II to provide low-cost home heating oil to poor families in Massachusetts. Citizens Energy helps the poor through a network of for-profit subsidiaries, i.e., money-making businesses that yield profits through commercial activity in the international oil market and in other energy-related industries. For example, the Citizens Energy Natural Gas Assistance Program uses net revenues from the sale of natural gas to local utilities to create assistance funds for the utilities' low-income customers. Citizens Energy is a nonprofit that actually owns a for-profit, taxable holding company consisting of successful business enterprises.

In 1983, Citizens decided that it could better serve the needy if it could actually generate revenue. Today, Citizens Corporation, the for-profit holding company that coordinates Citizens Energy's commercial activities, is a taxable entity that encompasses operations in crude oil, natural gas, electrical power marketing, and brokerage of mail-service pharmaceuticals. On the cutting edge of the utilities industry, it often finds itself brokering complex deals to transport megawatts of power across state lines through new arrangements and partnerships. The Citizens corporations include Citizens Gas Supply, now one of the largest independent marketers of natural gas in the nation, with an expanding base of gathering systems and storage facilities; Citizen's Power and Light, the country's first independent electrical power marketer; and Citizens Medical, a nationwide broker of mail-order pharmaceuticals.

By 1993 the *Boston Globe* reported that seven for-profit subsidiaries were contributing 40 percent of their profits to Citizens Energy, which spent the money on social programs both in the

United States and overseas, on projects as diverse as free fuel oil for homeless shelters to agricultural assistance in Africa. Since 1979 the company has distributed more than $33 million to such programs. As Joe Kennedy's brother Michael Kennedy, the current chairman and chief executive, told the *Boston Globe:* "What we were trying to do, at the end of the day, is create more competition and use our profits for something other than personal gain."

• Perhaps the most well known example of a Community Wealth Enterprise is Paul Newman's food company, Newman's Own, which donates 100 percent of after-tax profits to a wide array of charitable and educational causes. Beginning with salad dressing and then expanding to spaghetti sauces, popcorn, lemonade, and salsa, since 1982 his donations have totaled more than $60 million. For years Newman had packaged homemade salad dressing in wine bottles for Christmas gifts. On a lark, he and a friend decided to market the dressing and founded a small bottling company in Boston to distribute it locally. It was so popular that they ended up approaching a professional food broker that set up a network of fifty-six sub-brokers nationwide to sell and distribute to all of the top supermarket chains. Today, Newman's Own all-natural food products are distributed throughout the United States, and internationally to countries including Japan, Canada, Hong Kong, France, Germany, and Brazil, just to name a few. The concept is straightforward. In Newman's own words: "We furnish people with wholesome food that they enjoy, which then enables us to take the profits we make and give them to the unfortunate people of the country, who, because of poverty, sickness, old age, or illiteracy, desperately need help."

Under the motto of "Shameless exploitation in pursuit of the common good," the programs he supports include medical and health-related causes, substance-abuse programs, the environment, the arts, and the American Red Cross's emergency-relief efforts in Rwanda. Organizations such as the National Wildlife Federation, Habitat for Humanity, United Negro College Fund, and the Council on Literacy have all benefited from Newman's vision of a business as Community Wealth Enterprise.

A typical recipient, one that qualifies as an organization outside the mainstream, would be the Careers Through Culinary Arts Programs, which teaches at-risk youth culinary skills and guides them in seeking careers in food service while also working to build self-esteem and keep participants in school. The program currently operates one hundred fifty schools around the United States. Another project particularly close to Newman's heart is the Hole in the Wall Gang Camp, which he founded in 1988 for children with cancer and other serious blood-related illness.

This Community Wealth Enterprise won Newman his third Oscar™ in 1994, when he was awarded the Jean Hersholt Humanitarian Award by the Motion Picture Academy for the more than $56 million he'd donated at that time.

• Working Assets is a privately held, socially responsible long-distance, credit card, and travel services company that contributes 1 percent of long-distance revenues (as opposed to profits) to a variety of nonprofit organizations. It was started by Laura Scher, a Harvard Business School graduate, in 1985. By 1994 its projected revenues were exceeding $55 million, $4.5 million of which had been contributed to groups working for peace, human rights, economic justice, and a clean environment. The nonprofits, which have included Planned Parenthood, the Children's Defense Fund, Oxfam America, and Amnesty International, are nominated by its 300,000 customers, who then vote on how to distribute the funds. Scher explains, "Social change is our reason for being. Profit is simply a means to that end." The strategy seems to be working. In 1993 Working Assets was named one of the five hundred fastest-growing privately held companies by *Inc.* magazine.

The entrepreneurs who have founded and run the companies in each of these cases established a business enterprise with products and services designed to meet consumer demand regardless of the consumer's charitable intentions. The only thing truly different about these companies from their competitors in the marketplace is what they have choosen to do with their profits and the role that played in motivating them to begin their company in the first place.

There are also Community Wealth Enterprises that began as nonprofits and subsequently developed business strategies to generate revenue. Share Our Strength is a good example.

While legally and theoretically a nonprofit, Share Our Strength in practice is more like the hybrid of for-profit and nonprofit mentioned above. Although about one-third of our revenues derive from grassroots events that raise charitable dollars, another side of SOS is actively involved in creating new wealth. We do it by providing marketing and promotional advantages to corporate partners who *contract* with us for such services. We also create and sell products like books, jewelry, and other merchandise. Share Our Strength's efforts add to the gross national product and create jobs just like any other small business.

Another example of a nonprofit developing for-profit revenue streams is City Year, established in 1988 by Alan Khazei and Michael Brown, two Harvard Law School graduates, and initially funded through foundation and government grants. City Year is the Boston-based national youth corps that taps the idealism of young people to meet community needs. It served as a model for President Clinton's national service initiative, Americorps. The Timberland shoe company began supporting City Year in 1989, when it provided boots to corps members. Together they are now producing and selling City Year Gear, a line of apparel and accessories, ranging from T-shirts to backpacks, that promote positive messages of hope. Up to seventeen of Timberland's retail stores will have special display tables and educational materials about City Year and the City Year–Timberland partnership.

What's important about this initiative is not only that it will help generate funds for City Year's growth while increasing financial flexibility; it also is designed to increase the financial returns and strategic position of Timberland. In 1992, Timberland's "Give Racism the Boot" international advertising campaign generated awareness for Timberland worldwide and customers proved eager to purchase T-shirts, pins, and buttons with the campaign's message on them. Timberland has been looking for new products that speak more directly to young consumers and at a lower cost. Its own carefully conducted in-store research confirms that Timberland customers are an attractive target for "belief-based" products.

❧

Harvard professor Michael Porter has studied the social consequences of the poverty of America's inner cities. In the May-June 1995 issue of the *Harvard Business Review* he describes how past efforts to restore the inner city through relief programs like food stamps have failed, and calls for a radically different approach focused on creating a sustainable economic base that will permit inner-city businesses and employment opportunities for inner-city residents to proliferate and grow.

Porter acknowledges that change will not come easily. Re-thinking issues "in economic rather than social terms will be un-comfortable for many who have devoted years to social causes and who view profit and business in general with suspicion. Ac-tivists accustomed to lobbying for more government resources will find it difficult to embrace a strategy for wealth creation." Indeed, as Porter points out, nonprofits and community-based organizations focused on economic development in the inner city have a dismal record in running for-profit businesses. With the exception of low-income housing development, from which private contractors enjoy massive public subsidies, the majority of such businesses have failed. Most inner-city community-based nonprofits lack the skills, resources, training, and back-grounds necessary to create successful businesses. Porter argues that they also lack the attitude and incentives necessary to suc-ceed, but here I disagree. What Porter sees as an obstacle war-ranting surrender I view as an educational battle to be waged and won. The motivation and incentive of public-service entre-preneurs are just as strong as those of businesspeople in the for-profit community. Indeed they've typically pursued their objectives at great sacrifice and against great odds and can be counted on to adapt to new strategies if convinced of their effec-tiveness.

What he details for the inner city is equally true for the non-profit community at large: a sustainable economic base can be created "only as it has been created elsewhere: through private, for-profit initiatives and investment based on economic self-interest and genuine competitive advantage—not through artificial inducements, charity, or government mandates. . . . Our policies and programs have fallen into the trap of redistributing wealth. The real need—and the real opportunity—is to create wealth."

Community Wealth Enterprises by themselves can't solve every problem confronting society but they do add a powerful new weapon to the arsenals of community activists, volunteers, change advocates, and nonprofit executives. This model can have an impact far beyond hunger and poverty. It can be useful to organizations dealing with AIDS, the environment, medical research, literacy, domestic violence, and many other issues.

Another dozen Community Wealth Enterprises like Newman's Own Fine Foods would yield nearly a billion dollars for community needs. If the 499 other Fortune 500 companies had $6 million partnerships with Community Wealth Enterprises, as American Express has with Share Our Strength, another $3 billion could be devoted to alleviating the impact of poverty and creating change. Community Wealth Enterprises represent a new option that can revolutionize nonprofit work in the challenging times ahead by supporting a wide range of social programs and community services that are starved for resources. CWEs can be a powerful new tool for building community wealth, making new resources available for social services, and allowing talented business entrepreneurs to contribute more to society. They can also provide a readily accessible means for concerned citizens to assume greater civic responsibility, thereby enabling us to become fluent in the language of community.

6

"Something we were withholding made us weak
Until we found out it was ourselves
We were withholding from our land of living,
And forthwith found salvation in surrender.
Such as we were we gave ourselves outright"

ROBERT FROST,
from "The Gift Outright,"
read at the inauguration
of President John F. Kennedy

From the front door of my home in Silver Spring, Maryland, it's only about sixty-five miles to a small white church that sits on a slight hill overlooking one of the most beautiful and peaceful landscapes on the continent. The church is called the Dunker Church, and through its windows you can see a pasture, formerly a cornfield, where a battle was fought that in one day took a human toll never exceeded by any other in United States history. Of all the days in all of the places where American soldiers have fought, none was more terrible than September 17, 1862, at Antietam Creek.

Union losses were more than 12,400 that day. Confederate losses topped 10,700. One soldier recalled that at the peak of the fighting, it seemed, in his mind's eye, as if "the landscape turned red." But the record number of men killed and wounded at Antietam is not its only historical significance. The battle's outcome halted Robert E. Lee's invasion of the North. Victory here gave President Lincoln the opportunity he'd long been seeking to issue the Emancipation Proclamation, announced just five days after the battle, which declared free all slaves in states still in rebellion against the United States. It was a bold move and it suddenly gave the war a new, dual purpose: To preserve the Union and to end slavery.

It seems uncomfortably trite to say that too many Americans today still aren't free, that the poverty that traps nearly 40 million Americans has never been fought as boldly or with the same sense of purpose that Lincoln pursued his cause. But you simply can't spend an afternoon by the swift, shallow waters of Antietam Creek without stopping to wonder about the kinds of things Americans today would really put themselves on the line for, and if the complex matrix of hunger, homelessness, crime, illiteracy, and other issues that both derive from and perpetuate poverty could someday become the target of a sustained and unified national commitment.

President Reagan liked to quip that in the 1960s we waged a war on poverty and poverty won. It was a quip that struck a nerve in liberals and conservatives alike who could not fail to be disappointed that the government's efforts did not have a more profound and permanent impact. But there was, and is, at least one significant element missing from the battles of that war that distinguishes it from other wars waged throughout history. That missing element is us.

Wars are won by people. Not by money, or machinery, or even by strategy, but rather by the commitment and quality of the troops in the field. This is a basic tenet of military doctrine, whether modern or traditional. And it must be a basic tenet of the strategy to fight poverty and rebuild community. Creating community wealth is one component of that strategy. Matching it with the expenditure of a new community currency that targets personal skills, talents, and strengths at specific community needs is the second part of the battle plan.

The recent history of American politics and social change is a history of looking to others to solve our problems, of investing them with our trust and confidence and our votes. That of course is part and parcel of democracy, and as a political system it would be hard to improve upon. But some of our problems are larger than our political system, larger than our politicians, their parties, and the institutions they've created. Those problems need to be addressed by more than just politicians. We have got to use our own hands and hearts and minds to build the communities we want for our children. Politicians can't legislate it all for us. We need to take the radically democratic step of putting our trust and confidence back in ourselves.

The professional politicians in Washington—whether Democrats or Republicans—do not see us as part of a new strategy. Instead they rehash sterile arguments and offer false choices instead of new possibilities. Nowhere is this more evident than in the debate triggered by House Speaker Newt Gingrich's proposal to replace the social service and welfare programs that have been in place since Lyndon Johnson's Great Society with private voluntary charity. On a number of occasions Speaker Gingrich has tried to rationalize drastic cuts in social services by stating, "I believe we should have a conscious strategy of dramatically increasing private charities. I believe that private charities are more effective, they are less expensive, and they are better for the people they are helping."

A statement like this requires a high-octane blend of ignorance and arrogance, but Speaker Gingrich has managed it. In the short term, his policies are simply wrong because all hard evidence pertaining to private charity compensating for federal budget cuts points to the contrary. Independent Sector, a national clearinghouse of information regarding charities, has projected the impact of the proposed cuts on a sample of more than one hundred nonprofits ranging from nursing homes and Head Start programs to colleges and disaster-relief agencies. Their contributions would have to more than double over the next seven years for them to make up for the proposed cuts. Even in the best of times, the increase in donations for charities from year to year is only 5 percent. The financing of anti-hunger efforts serves as a good example of what this means in real terms. The federal government spends $39 billion a year on food assistance programs. That includes food stamps, school lunch, and school breakfast programs, and the Women, Infants, and Children supplemental feeding programs—$39 billion! Foundation, corporate, and private charitable dollars fighting hunger add up to less than $4 billion annually. If the Gingrich cuts were enacted, millions more poor children and their families would end up staring at empty tables despite charity's best efforts to close some of the $35 billion gap.

Speaker Gingrich's budget cuts would not just shrink the federal government, they would shrink nonprofit and charitable services as well, and just at the time when the demand for them would be heavier than ever. Many of the programs Gingrich would cut provide critical financial resources to support and strengthen the very charitable efforts he claims society should rely upon instead of government. The infrastructure for non-profit efforts focusing on food assistance, housing, job training, education, helping dislocated workers find new jobs, and many other social services is built with federal dollars.

Still, if there's one thing worse than being wrong, it's being irrelevant. In the long-term Gingrich's policies will turn out to be both. The declining state of intellectual ferment in American politics allows the Contact with America to be viewed as a bold document by its Republicans sponsors and Democratic adversaries alike. There's nothing new or revolutionary about budget reductions, the death penalty, product liability law reform, cutting capital gains taxes, and other provisions of the Contract. It is a cut-and-paste rehash of unimaginative ideas that have commanded knee-jerk Republican support and appealed to special interest groups for years. The so-called Republican Revolution is more like a timid, cowering surrender to the intractable social problems of the 1990s. With the context and perspective that only time and history can provide, the Republican takeover of Congress in 1994 will be seen as the beginning of a new cycle that transformed electoral politics, but not American society.

If the Republicans are both wrong and irrelevant, the Democrats are in the not very useful position of being right but irrelevant. Democrats are right in declaring that the cuts in social services will hurt people and should be resisted. But their stance on maintaining the status quo won't create change. The aim of even the most expansive Democratic vision is expanded government programs. Increasing funding to extend benefit eligibility to more people only brings more people into a system that is not working.

This is not intended as an anti-government polemic, however. I worked in government long enough to know government can save lives, make it possible for a child to get educated or a grandparent to have health care, and create opportunities for families and businesses to grow strong enough so that government support becomes unnecessary. It just can't do it all by itself. If Senator Bill Bradley is right in saying that government and the market are two legs of a three-legged stool made unstable without the third leg of a strong, responsible citizenry, then government money must be matched by an expenditure of what I call community currency, people sharing their strengths and skills directly with others in need. If anything, the new strategy proposed here will protect and preserve government's role while giving way to more realistic expectations about what government has the capacity to do. At the same time, this strategy will see the growth of new resources that will help relieve government by shouldering a portion of the load.

In William Safire's anthology of great speeches, one Rabbi Louis Finkelstein of the Jewish Theological Seminary in New York tells of a conversation the Roman emperor Hadrian had with a Jewish sage named Y'Hoshua Ben Chananyah in the year A.D. 130, when Rome was at the height of its power. Rabbi Y'Hoshua foresaw the decline of the Roman empire as a result of the barbarians, as they were called, who were taken captive by Rome and trained as soldiers to hold back other barbarians. It was only a matter of time, he predicted, before these barbarians would go over to their brother barbarians and attack Rome, which actually happened within 250 years.

"He was trying to say to the Roman emperor," Rabbi Finkelstein speculated, "that the very survival of Roman civilization depended on a shift in policy—that they had come to the end of what could be done with arms. Therefore he believed that Rome had to bring to its policy a new idea, the idea of brotherhood. . . . The emperor could not accept this, because in order to accept it he would have had to change not Roman policy but Roman character." Just as Rome came to the end of what could be done with arms, our social programs have come to the end of what can be done with money. We need not just changes in national policy, but changes in character.

Community currency may sound like an abstract term for volunteerism or community service or the kinds of "points of light" activities President Bush once celebrated. But that is not what it means. And those doing it need not be volunteers. The key is for social programs to include personal involvement, whether voluntary or paid. Geoffrey Canada, president of Harlem's Rheedlen Center, who works full-time alongside children on dangerous streets, maintains that "the problem cannot be solved from afar." Having spent years knocking on doors by day to round up kids late for school and walking the streets at night, negotiating with gangs, he insists, "You have to make a commitment to stick with them for years."

These sentiments are echoed by Barry Kelly, a retired CIA officer who has been a tutor and mentor for four years in Washington's I Have a Dream project, which pays for a student's college tuition if he or she makes it through high school. The program includes comprehensive tutoring and mentoring, family counseling, and extracurricular activities. Kelly states, "The problem in the inner city is not money. The problem is people. You need that person-to-person commitment. If we had one hundred churches down here, we could make a difference." Similarly, a $1 million experiment financed by the Ford Foundation, known as the Quantum Opportunities Program, broke sharply with a generation of programs aimed at the specific problems of poor youths—teenage pregnancy, delinquency, failure at school, and unemployment—to build a program based on the philosophy that what poor children from dissolved families need most is an adult who cares about them and stays by them for years.

A broad study of hundreds of anti-poverty efforts across the United States by Jonathan Freedman, author of *From Cradle to Grave: The Human Face of Poverty in America,* bears this out. "The ultimate value of a particular program was not in its overt reason for being, but for the fact that it provided a way for two people—one in need of help and another wanting to help—to form a bond transforming both their lives. If there is a railing to help people, it will be made up of not just government programs or private efforts, but of human hands. It takes money, organization, and laws to maintain a social structure, but none of it works if there are not opportunities for people to meet and help each other along the way. . . . The most basic level of response is not governmental; it is intimate, one on one, neighbor to neighbor, family to family, community by community, hand by hand, until the railing is within our grasp."

So how can individuals spend community currency? One example is a program pioneered by Share Our Strength called Operation Frontline. It is a private corps of chefs and restaurateurs trained to serve at maternal and child health clinics and community centers, where they teach low-income families nutrition, cooking, budgeting, and grocery-shopping skills— essential ingredients to fighting hunger effectively. Moving chefs from their restaurant to the front line in the fight against hunger connects those who know the most about food and nutrition with those who have the greatest need for this information. Typically these types of services would be left to social workers or government employees, but the passion and enthusiasm the chefs have for food is contagious and far more effective than telling low-income families, "This is what the government says is good for you to eat." They are natural teachers, with daily experience teaching their own kitchen staffs how to prepare and serve. Operation Frontline chefs are speaking the language of community. As Maria Gomez, the director of Washington, D.C.'s Mary's Center, one of the family centers hosting the program, explained, "After the program got under way we sometimes couldn't locate the women who use our center at the times we usually found them at home. Then we discovered that, for the first time, they were in each other's homes, cooking together. Operation Frontline not only taught skills, it built community." Another Frontline coordinator found that what the participants liked most was being involved in learning again, so they now invite graduate equivalency diploma and continuing education counselors to the last class to enroll participants in other community education efforts.

Other professions have similar capabilities. In Richmond,

Virginia, a theater company called Theater IV has been using humor and drama to teach kids about drug addiction, teenage pregnancy, and sexual abuse. The vision of the founders was to use the stage to bring about social change. So far the group has performed in schools, theaters, and hospitals in thirty-seven states. Likewise, the trumpeter Wynton Marsalis has visited more than one thousand schools over the past decade to teach young people about jazz. He was quoted in *Life* magazine as saying, "What a kid learns from jazz is how to express his individuality without stepping on somebody else's. The first thing I tell kids is, 'Play anything you want but make it sound like you.' The next step is learning to control that self-expression. Don't just blurt something out, adapt it to what the other guy is doing. Being a good neighbor, that's what jazz is all about. Jazz is democracy in action." Teaching jazz is teaching the language of community.

Imagine what today's entrepreneurs leading the information and telecommunications revolution would have to offer beyond donations and grants to charitable institutions. Their leadership can contribute their special technical knowledge and creativity to devise ways in which the information revolution can deliver services to those hardest to reach but most in need of help. The possibilities range from introducing basic instructional materials into every home regarding nutrition, literacy, and prenatal care to equipping home health care providers with handheld computers that relay medical information back and forth, to international teleconferences among the indigenous peoples of the world. Technology, when properly applied, can yield more than profitable new forms of shopping and entertainment.

Child immunization is a good example. Less than half of all young children in the United States are properly vaccinated. Expense, lack of access, and elaborate record-keeping systems are obstacles to thorough immunization. Parents lose or misplace records. Health care providers don't know who needs shots and who doesn't. The Clinton administration plans a computerized national registry for tracking and keeping records on children's immunizations. It is long overdue, even though the technology has long been available to the private sector. Anyone who has ever used Federal Express or UPS knows that small handheld computers enable any employee in the system to tell you exactly where your package is at any time. Immunizations are packages, too—packages of medicine—but we have no idea which have reached their destinations and which have not. Sadly, not one social service in this country is delivered with the efficiency and accountability of a Federal Express package.

Of course dollars matter. Vital forms of support and important services cannot be delivered without them. But if you stop to listen, each day brings fresh voices expressing a new realization that decisions about allocating federal and state dollars will only be effective if matched by a commitment to allocate community currency as well.

No amount of money can substitute for personal involvement. That's not to say that social programs don't have costs and need financing. They do. But the essential ingredients are not dollars, grants, stipends, or government contracts. The essential ingredients are people who are willing to go to neighborhoods not their own, to work with people not like them, and to share the strengths and skills and attitudes that have enabled them to be successful in their own lives.

Let's be clear about what is being suggested. Does this mean we need to turn our lives upside down, sell our homes, and move into these neighborhoods in pursuit of some Utopian dream? Should Capitol Hill's policy makers move across the river to Anacostia? Should Wall Street brokers pick up and relocate to Harlem? Of course that is not about to happen. But we better find the next best way for our diverse societies, cultures, and peoples to come into contact with each other.

Like the currency of a nation that has been devalued one too many times, a new currency is now being sought in our most troubled communities. The savvy and streetwise know the old stuff just isn't worth what it used to be and that they need to be trading in a new currency. Dollars alone—whether federal, state, or local—don't have the buying power they once did. The outcomes we desire for our children and our inner cities can't be purchased through the spending of taxpayer dollars. Taxpayers need to spend their time as well. And their energy, skills, hope, and inspiration.

Community Wealth Enterprises and other established charitable organizations like Share Our Strength will continue to expand rapidly in the months ahead. More money will be raised. Many millions of dollars more. Some of the most basic humanitarian needs of the most vulnerable in our society will be met. But how will we turn the corner? No matter how hard we work we can't "out-fund-raise" hunger and poverty. Indeed, no social condition, no tide of history, has ever been reversed just as a result of superior fund-raising.

If we are going to create lasting change, it will be because we change the way people think about themselves and their responsibilities and their opportunities to contribute to the greater good of their community. It will be because we set an example so powerful, so compelling, and so clearly understood that its story is repeated over and over again—through the press, through word of mouth, through the pulpit, and through the schools—until it receives widespread acceptance in the public consciousness.

One of Gandhi's biographers explained that the strategy behind Gandhi's use of civil disobedience for the seemingly impossible objective of gaining India's independence from the British empire was that he "sought to create a story, a conception, a way of being that could make sense to every other individual irrespective of his or her particular history or craft. Difficult as it is to change a domain, it is far more challenging to create a new human narrative and to render it convincingly to other individuals."

So how do we create a new human narrative? How will we get a society to think differently and bravely about ending poverty, about not leaving people behind? How do we get our friends and neighbors to realize that the responsibility for solving some of our most pressing problems is not just government's or charity's or someone else's, but our own? How do we create a narrative in which one of life's rites of passage is about putting not just our wallets on the line, but ourselves as well?

The answer lies in the only thing we haven't tried: a massive, nationwide commitment of talented, compassionate, and creative people in our society, a commitment not only to support worthwhile programs and projects financially, but rather to deploy skills and special talents on behalf of people in need, *personally.* The effort must be focused, sophisticated, organized, and directed toward the toughest tasks, rather than the tasks that are simply the most suitable for untrained but well-meaning volunteers. Just as we can't buy our way out of poverty, we can't volunteer our way out, either. Communities will be transformed only when the people in and around them are transformed. Electoral revolutions will be ephemeral, and in the long term irrelevant, unless the next American revolution is a revolution of the heart, a revolution within each and every one of us.

7

*The history of modern art, from Picasso's scrambled faces to
Andy Warhol's soup cans and beyond, is a recurrent pattern of
impertinent individual acts of imagination initiated with no
supporting consensus—new languages of expression that had
only the tiniest circle of initial understanding but which
produced the broadest conceivable changes in our way of
looking at and thinking about the world, and in the way we
represent life to ourselves.*

KIRK VARNADOE
curator,
Museum of Modern Art

Community Wealth Enterprises and community currency are the two components of a new strategy. Strategies are used to win wars. Tactics are used to win
battles. This chapter is about tactics.

Battles are being waged every day at schools, hospitals, playgrounds, and housing tenements to save the lives of children living under an unprecedented assault from ravages of poverty,
such as guns, drugs, gangs, and parental neglect. Success in

changing the way America defends its children will require new tactics to ensure that the community institutions fighting those battles have the resources they need to win. And since rebuilding community depends not just on our political leaders but on all of us, these tactics must be shared and understood by every citizen: officeholder, teacher, small-business owner, corporate executive, and community organization; by private entrepreneurs and public-interest entrepreneurs alike. Like any new effort still in its infancy, the lessons learned need to be refined, improved upon, and passed along.

Much of the nonprofit community exists as small, community-based organizations that have little or no contact with each other, or with similar organizations around the country that may have preceded or succeeded them. They do not enjoy the benefits of national leadership or coordination. Useful ideas developed by one organization are often unknown and not utilized by other organizations. In the for-profit sector of our economy, when someone builds a better mousetrap, the resources and the infrastructure exist to replicate it in every neighborhood. Whether it's Baskin-Robbins ice cream, The Body Shop, or H & R Bloch, successful companies find the venture capital and the technical expertise to replicate, franchise, and expand. No such help is available to an innovative new nonprofit concept, even one demonstrating concrete results and impact. Every community has its success story—a school or housing project or health clinic that works and has won widespread support—but the success rarely spreads further than that community. As Community Wealth Enterprises develop and flourish it would stand to reason that because they are creating new wealth, they would likely be eligible for loans, capital, and the investment necessary to expand. At this early stage, however, the best that can be done is to share strategies I've learned along the way that may help others to succeed.

The twelve basic principles below represent a road map of sorts for navigating this new territory. They can be applied directly to efforts to strengthen nonprofit organizations and other community-based organizations and particularly to building Community Wealth Enterprises. But they also have much broader application. They should be of use to anyone involved in selling, persuading, marketing, advocacy, coalition building, business, communications, and consulting. This chapter concludes with specific practical suggestions for those who want to get personally involved in creating the kind of community wealth that brings about meaningful change. An appendix in the back of this book lists a selective sampling of worthy existing organizations and addresses and phone numbers where they can be contacted.

1. YOUR MONEY OR YOUR LIFE.

Most good causes share one bad habit: asking for money. This is not a facetious complaint but rather an observation about the narrow manner by which many worthy causes seek support. Those who raise money—whether for the arts, the environment, or the poor—usually solicit the same people over and over again. But soon they grow weary of asking for money and the contributors grow weary of being asked. "Donor fatigue" eventually takes its toll and contributions dry up. Whether the hook is a fancy ballroom dinner or a slick direct-mail package, checks are written and all too frequently forgotten, and there is often little or no personal connection between the donor and the cause. One way of creating that connection is to ask individuals to contribute skills instead of checks.

The first important lesson learned at SOS was that chefs would rather donate $500 to $1,000 worth of food and an evening of their time preparing it at a benefit to fight hunger than put a check for $100 in the mail once a year. Personal participation at the events helped them feel connected to the cause and made their contribution more meaningful. This was reinforced when writers jumped at the chance to contribute their writing to the anthologies we published. Likewise with artists, photographers, musicians, and others. Corporate executives at American Express and other companies with whom we've negotiated marketing and promotional partnerships have made their greatest contribution by staying involved with the organization to share their skills in strategic planning, marketing, message development, and communications—areas of expertise we lacked and which they were generous to share, connecting them to our work in ways that a financial contribution never could.

When you've got their creative passion, you've got their hearts and minds—the best they have to give. Their checkbooks will follow. One contributor to *Louder Than Words* sends $5,000 every December without ever being asked, and many other contributors remain generous supporters in their own ways.

Comedian Jack Benny's classic joke about the robber who demanded, "Your money or your life," to which the notoriously stingy Benny replied, "I'm thinking, I'm thinking," comes to mind. When Share Our Strength can choose between asking someone for money or the product of their life's work, we choose the latter. Because of this, supporters are also more likely to spread the word about our work and recruit additional contributors. When a group of the nation's most talented chefs get together, how likely is it that they'll talk about their response to a direct-mail solicitation? On the other hand, the odds are much better that they'll talk about what they cooked at a recent food-and-wine benefit. This peer-to-peer influence and camaraderie can have a greater influence on others in the industry than anything a nonprofit organizer could do or say.

Every collaboration that taps into creative skills and talents will spawn another one that could not have been foreseen. A contributor to one book will have an idea for the next book, as did Michael J. Rosen, a prolific author and the literary director of Thurber House in Columbus, Ohio, who, after donating a verse to SOS's first anthology, proposed a series of children's books, which he then edited for us. Another contributor, Colgate professor Fred Busch, conceived and helped organize the Writers Harvest readings, in which hundreds of writers across the country read from their work to raise funds. A company that donates product to one event will have an idea for a promotion of its own, such as Fetzer Vineyards' production of 25,000 cases of a special-barrel select Chardonnay, whose SOS logo on the label yielded ten dollars a case for the organization.

Just as individuals with financial resources look for stocks, bonds, and other ways to invest, individuals with creative resources look for outlets in which to invest them. Every week at Share Our Strength brings unsolicited but welcome letters and calls from individuals with ideas for cookbooks, concerts, food products, CDs, sculptures, fashion items, and other revenue-generating ideas.

2. People Want to Be Part of Something Larger Than Themselves.

Creative individuals not only want to contribute through their skills, they want to be part of something larger than themselves. Regardless of the natural inclination to join a rolling bandwagon, there is a deeper sentiment involved. While holding Taste of the Nation events in one hundred cities at the same time could seem like a marketable gimmick, it is also a way of giving people a sense that they're a part of something bigger than just their own local event, that they are connected to others in an effort that reaches across the country.

Collective action is a strong and seductive motivator. It promises leverage, power in numbers. If people can see that their own contributions will be combined with those of an army of others, then value is added and the result can be more than the sum of its parts. This gives individuals a stronger incentive for contributing, and promises that their contribution will have an impact. Despair for our communities is of such a magnitude that people are naturally skeptical as to whether their contribution will make a difference. Being able to demonstrate that their support will be enhanced by the cumulative efforts of tens of thousands of others can be the strongest selling point for overcoming these doubts.

Finally, the economies of scale in organizing massive grassroots participatory activities have their advantages: Once the organizing infrastructure has been created, the marginal cost of organizing an individual event or selling an additional product goes down. Consequently, the profit margin on each incremental addition goes up. This is a fundamental principle of business that needs to be practiced by nonprofits as well as Community Wealth Enterprises.

3. LOCATION, LOCATION, LOCATION.

As anyone in real estate knows, the three most important factors in making a sale are location, location, location. The same holds true in building support for an idea. The best location to build support is the intersection of private interest and public interest.

All of Share Our Strength's fund-raising programs are consciously designed to ensure that our contributors get back something of value in addition to the psychic rewards of doing good. For example, the more than 60,000 patrons of our food-and-wine benefits receive the value of sampling the specialties of the best chefs in their community. Many of these people come because they care about the issue of hunger. Some come because they are devotees of fine food and wine. Either way is fine from our point of view. On the other side are the chefs and restaurateurs who participate in these benefits. By donating their food, supplies, and time, they get valuable visibility, free advertising and marketing benefits, and good public relations. Large corporate partners such as American Express, Martell Cognac, and Starbucks Coffee get access to marketing opportunities with restaurants that would not be available to them any other way. Promising intangible benefits like "good public image" and "consumer goodwill" are not enough anymore. Partners need to get specific and quantifiable benefits to sustain a long-term relationship.

Most nonprofit organizations eventually run low on gas. The engine of economic self-interest almost never does. Charitable intentions change or are fulfilled. The profit motive remains. A concrete example of how SOS has used this to its advantage is in the dozen books we've published to raise funds and awareness. We don't ask publishers to publish a book to help our organization or to give us all of their profits. Instead we accept the royalties the authors have donated and ask only that the publisher buy and publish the book on the same terms they would buy and publish any other book: that it is a product of quality and commercially viable. If the book sells, it's a win-win situation: SOS and the publisher make money.

4. Ask Not What Your Partners Can Do for You, Ask What You Can Do for Your Partners.

If substantial financial resources are to be raised and sustained over a long period of time, it's essential that supportive partners, especially large corporate partners, get as well as give.

To find the intersection of public interest and private interest that will work for your partners, begin by sitting down with them to learn about *their* needs before telling them about yours. What are their marketing and sales challenges? What specific public relations messages do they hope to convey? Who are their principal competitors and on what playing fields are they competing? How do they hope this partnership will be viewed by their employee workforce? Then go back and brainstorm so that you can return to the table with creative ideas for vehicles that will both raise money for and increase awareness of your cause, but will also meet the business needs of your partner. This ensures a partnership will live up to the truest definition of the word, and increases the likelihood that the relationship will be a long-lasting one. When you are asking people to buy something that they might want or need, you are in a stronger position than when you are simply asking them to give you something for nothing beyond the warm feeling of giving.

Every potential corporate partner you meet is approached

by dozens of other organizations representing worthy causes. Whether it's the environment, AIDS, or legal services for the poor, you can assume that like you, they'll have a prestigious board of directors, impressive annual reports, touching anecdotes about how their work has changed lives. Why should a corporation's senior management choose your idea over another? The competitive edge will be yours if what you have to offer your corporate partner is good for them. Make sure it is.

Keep in mind that a corporation, no matter how large, is the individuals with whom you are working. These people are accountable to their superiors and they are expected to produce. If you can help them accomplish that, then yours will be a long and profitable relationship.

A tip on a frequently overlooked angle: It is often better to approach a corporate partner through one of the agencies they have retained to represent them for public relations, advertising, or marketing than to proceed directly to the company. Every large corporation has multiple agencies, and these agencies have people trained and hired for their ability to identify and communicate creative opportunities in the interest of the companies they represent. Whether it is Ogilvy & Mather on behalf of IBM or Hill & Knowlton on behalf of Procter & Gamble, the agency staff is likely to be a receptive port of entry. There is not nearly as much competition for the ear of the right person. Another potential benefit is that since agencies represent many companies, they may be able to help you with their other clients in the future.

Finally, your partners not only need to get something out of the relationship, they need *to know* they are getting something. Don't assume they will see the benefits on their own. Instead, identify them, measure them, quantify them, and communicate them. Also, make sure your partners not only hear from you, but from their customers, other local businessmen, and civic leaders enjoying the benefits of a revitalized community, who made that work possible. This way your partners can see that it's been good for their standing in the community and consequently for their business.

Your partners are not in a position to measure the impact their dollars have had on your program. You are. If the work is successful, it's going to make them feel good for playing a part in it, but only if they know about it. Communicate more than numbers. Communicate the impact on people's lives. Take partners to see a family or a health clinic or a school breakfast program that benefited from your work. Self-interest is powerful, but not as powerful as self-interest matched with idealism. Give your partners access to both.

5. Make It Your Business.

It's easier to work with a business, and more likely that you will, if you are run like a business yourself.

A gulf exists today between the private for-profit community and the nonprofit sector. They don't understand our work nor do we understand theirs. They don't do their work as we do ours. Senior corporate executives who are highly educated, sophisticated, well traveled, and knowledgeable about the ways of the world in virtually every other aspect of their lives often lack experience with public policy issues. Likewise, the staffs of nonprofits and Community Wealth Enterprises who are likely to be on the cutting edge of social and political change often can't read a balance statement, don't measure and quantify the impact of their efforts, and have little access to or practical experience with state-of-the-art communications and marketing ideas. Community Wealth Enterprises represent an opportunity to bridge this gulf for the purpose of bringing enormous resources to bear on important social problems.

Running your organization like a business need not mean adopting stereotypical corporate values that place making money ahead of social change and human values. But what it can mean is using the techniques that businesses have developed to enhance the appeal and advance the promotion of their products or services. Most of these are so conventional in the corporate world that they are taken for granted: a long-term strategic plan, an analysis of profit centers and cost centers, targeted advertising, focus groups, survey research, incentive programs, etc.

American entrepreneurial ingenuity has a long history of developing methods of better communication, more efficient management, and more effective marketing. Why not take advantage of this rich legacy? Why reinvent the wheel or ignore wheels already invented?

6. SELL WHAT PEOPLE WANT TO BUY.

It's not enough to sell T-shirts and coffee mugs with your logo on them. A Community Wealth Enterprise needs to have a product or service that meets a specific demand. Paul Newman's food company is a terrific example. The customers for Paul Newman's products don't purchase them to please Paul Newman or to be associated with the causes he supports, but because his products satisfy a need and appetite independent of the consumer's charitable desires.

7. ROUND UP THE UNUSUAL SUSPECTS.

One of the most common failures of nonprofits and other enterprises is the failure to preach beyond the choir, to reach more than the converted. New and sustainable energy, financial resources, creativity, and talent all depend on continually bringing new people into the effort. Many fund-raising campaigns, particularly direct mail, are based on the premise that "no good deed should go unpunished," and so enormous energies are devoted to squeezing every last dollar out of a proven donor. Instead, the goal should be to create new donors.

Too many nonprofits try to come up with a niche that will enable them to get their piece of the pie, when what they should be doing is helping to make the pie larger by recruiting new supporters. This will alleviate competition with other organizations for the same small circle of charitable wealth.

There's no passion in the world to match that of a convert. They have no sense of limitation or of what can't be done. As a result they provide an energy and commitment that is often lacking from the trustworthy regulars. One of the Share Our Strength anthologies was a collection of science writing. Paleontologists, astrophysicists, and neuro-linguists aren't the first groups that come to mind when thinking about who can help generate resources for hungry children, but these scientists were delighted to find that their work could be converted into such resources. And because others had not already thought to connect them to a cause like ours, they were eager to help in an unpredictably enthusiastic way.

Everyone expects traditional liberal activists to be supporting social causes. But what does it say about an issue if you can bring to it businesspeople, scientists, and poets? This type of diversity among supporters not only yields additional resources, but also credibility, man-bites-dog-type press attention, and increased public interest.

8. LITTLE ACORNS AND GREAT OAKS.

The key to building a large partnership is beginning with a small partnership that, if successful, can grow. There is no such thing as too small in this regard. It is the only way to begin.

The largest cause-related marketing campaign in U.S. history began between Share Our Strength and American Express in 1990, when several restaurateurs who were SOS supporters and American Express customers suggested that American Express sign on as the exclusive national sponsor of Share Our Strength's Taste of the Nation benefits. They reasoned that the two organizations needed each other and that a partnership could be good for both. The sponsorship meant American Express would pay a fee to cover SOS's costs of putting on the food-and-wine benefit, and support other aspects of the organization's work. In return, the event would be known as "American Express Presents Taste of the Nation." American Express received a written guarantee that we would use our best efforts to ensure their visibility, advantageous positioning on signage, posters, invitations, etc. For American Express it was an opportunity to build better relationships with the more than five thousand chefs and restaurateurs participating in the food-and-wine event—the very people who decide whether or not to accept the American Express Card at their establishments. From the outset our objective was to ensure that American Express got out of the relationship what they needed, which was an opportunity to position and present themselves in support of something important to restaurant owners.

The response was so positive that American Express decided to maintain its sponsorship of Taste of the Nation on a multiyear basis. We invited American Express employees to the events, to our offices, to visit grant recipients so they could see how the event proceeds were being used, and to our regular conferences and meetings. American Express became part of the SOS family and developed closer relationships with their restaurant customers as well. Soon another division at the company, the student card division, contacted us about entering into a partnership with SOS, too. They had observed that their colleagues who worked on Taste of the Nation were doing well in the company and having fun while doing something with meaning and purpose. We created a new program with the student card division called the Million Meals campaign—that is, American Express agreed to make a contribution to SOS every time a student cardholder used his or her card for a specific period of time during the school year. One hundred thousand dollars were raised.

A year later I was contacted by John Pritchett, who was heading up a new division at American Express, whose goal was to devise incentives for cardholders to insist that their American Express card be accepted and used at service establishments that might otherwise "suppress" its use. Pritchett was hoping to develop a program that would unite all of the diverse elements of the company, while also responding to the interest expressed by American Express employees to be more involved in community. This would be much more than a cause-related marketing campaign; it would represent a total corporate commitment large enough to reduce hunger significantly in the United States as well as overcome the natural cynicism of the press and the public about such corporate efforts. He had heard good things about SOS from his colleagues, and his initial question was a provocative one: Would we know how to spend $15 million to $45 million over the next three years if we happened to receive that much?

Over the next three months we devised a campaign whose result would be a two cents' contribution to SOS every time the American Express card was used anywhere in the United States, for any reason, for the last three months of each year, a fourth-quarter period that includes the Christmas shopping and travel season. So far Charge Against Hunger has yielded more than $5 million for community-based anti-hunger organizations each year. The campaign was advertised on television and featured the work of SOS in a way that increased public awareness of SOS more than anything else in our organization's history.

American Express and Charge Against Hunger transformed Share Our Strength. Most gratifying of all was that many of the senior executives and staff of American Express became deeply committed to SOS and stayed involved even when their official job responsibilities at the company changed. Their contacts in the corporate world continue to help us expand in new directions. What began as a simple event sponsorship grew into an unprecedented national commitment that ultimately enabled SOS to build relationships with new partners ranging from Universal Studios and Northwest Airlines to K-Mart and This End Up.

9. Continuous Improvement Is Disastrous.

In a chapter from Tom Peters's seminar called "Toward Perpetual Revolution," the co-author of *In Search of Excellence* explains that "change and constant improvement, the watchwords of the eighties, are no longer enough." He quotes Paul O'Neil, the CEO of Alcoa, who believes that continuous improvement is "probably a disastrous idea if you are far behind the world standard." The same is true for nonprofits, at least those responsible for vitally needed social service. If the standard is eliminating poverty, then incremental progress will never be enough. "Continuous improvement" as an organization, usually considered laudatory and satisfying, will never get us to the goal. Only quantum leaps in the number of people we are able to serve and in the qualitative measures of that service, will produce the results we need.

The resources available for nonprofit work in this country are vast but often profoundly underestimated. By setting our sights too low we create self-fulfilling prophecies of scarcity and want. We condemn ourselves to making incremental progress against problems that are not growing incrementally, but rather exponentially.

At General Electric, one of America's largest and most successful companies, the chairman, John Welch, has instituted an operating principle called "stretch." He explains to shareholders that stretch is a concept that means "using dreams to set business targets—with no real idea of how to get there." Indeed, he says, "If you do know how to get there, it's not a stretch target." GE, he says, used to "timidly nudge the peanut along, setting goals of moving from, say, 4.73 percent inventory turns to 4.91 percent, or from 8.53 percent operating margin to 8.92 percent, and then indulge in time-consuming, high-level, bureaucratic negotiations to move the number a few hundredths one way or the other. The point is, it didn't matter." Incremental goals "inspire or challenge no one, capture no imaginations."

According to James Collins and Jerry Porras, the authors of *Built to Last,* instead of setting goals, visionary companies set BHAGs—Big Hairy Audacious Goals—challenges so clear and compelling that they focus and unify everyone around a common effort. Most nonprofits don't have the luxury of growing incrementally. The demands on them are too great. "Stretch thinking" and BHAGs inspire and stimulate the progress necessary to bring organizations closer to their true capacity.

10. "CENTER IT!" (THE LEIBOWITZ STRATEGY).

My son Zachary has played ice hockey since he was six years old. Because ice time is scarce in suburban Maryland, kids that age usually get the Sunday-morning, 7:00 A.M. time slots. They are oblivious to both the time and the cold, which cannot be said of their parents, dutifully cheering them on in the bleachers. These young boys are blessed with many coaches; in fact, each father fancies himself a coach and is usually available to shout from the bleachers or pound on the protective Plexiglas. Over the years it has become safe to generalize that the parents who are the loudest know the least about the game of hockey. The one exception to that rule was Alex Leibowitz's dad, an intense man with a big droopy mustache and a resonant, booming voice. Mr. Leibowitz would shout, *"Center it!"* whenever little Alex got anywhere near the puck. During every game Alex Leibowitz's father would yell, *"Center it, center it, Alex!"* over and over, so many times that it still rings in my ears to this day. I was often tempted to ask him if he could envision any set of circumstances on the ice in which it would not be appropriate for little Alex to "center it."

But Mr. Leibowitz's advice was sound and remarkably strategic. He was urging Alex to pass the puck to the center of the ice, where there would be a chance of someone who was better positioned to have a clear shot at the goal. With six-year-old boys it's every man for himself. Every kid who gets his stick on the puck tries to score right then and there, no matter where he is or how far from the goal. Six-year-old boys do not skate with the puck. They do not pass the puck. They do not assess the probabilities of success before they shoot the puck. As a result, they are only rarely successful in getting the puck to the goal. So one of the essential ingredients of teaching teamwork is teaching them first to center the puck.

The same is true of young and growing nonprofit organizations. If a nonprofit that had perfected a winning strategy could somehow "center" the concept so that other groups around the country could replicate it, well, goals could be scored. For example, an organization in Atlanta may have discovered the best way to ensure higher child immunization rates in the inner city, but there is little likelihood that they will be able to replicate their program in Philadelphia or Chicago. As a local organization they would not have access to funds beyond Atlanta. The social services landscape in America is overcrowded with good ideas that remain stranded in the place of their birth.

If organizations want to have a reach beyond their own territory, one of the most effective things they can do is develop a plan for "centering" their idea and making it available in a place others can find it. When Project Bread, a statewide anti-hunger group in Massachusetts, applied to SOS for a $100,000 grant, we told them we would more likely approve a grant for $110,000 that included a strategy of replication and technical assistance that would make their work accessible to other state organizations. Strategies for "centering it" must contain a replication component that includes technical assistance and travel teams but relies on local investment and indigenous local leadership to bring a new program to a new site.

11. WE HAVE MET THE ENEMY AND HE IS US.

One of the greatest problems faced by those seeking to create social change is the profound lack of public awareness and sophistication about what the real problems are. There is always enormous public sympathy and support for dealing with relief efforts, but not for prevention. Homeless families at Christmas, crack boarder babies, the dying child's last wish all win our sympathy. But there is rarely understanding and support for efforts to deal with the deeper underlying causes. These matters are often more complex, more controversial, and less amenable to the types of simple catchy slogans that motivate people to make charitable contributions. Too often nonprofits take the easy route of appealing to their sense of pity and charity, which brings in money but not much in the way of understanding. The real goal must be to fight poverty by addressing underlying issues such as education, job training, wage structures, economic development.

12. DO IT YOURSELF.

Here are a few practical, easy steps you can personally take that can put you at the forefront of community change:

• Create signature items through your business to support a good cause. The Dahlia Lounge restaurant in Seattle promises a dollar to SOS every time a customer purchases chef Tommy Douglas's signature pear tart. Similarly, you can identify a single item in your business, whether it's a pastry, a VCR, a running shoe, or an oil filter, whose purchase will benefit whatever cause is closest to your heart. It not only raises money and awareness of important community issues but gives your customers an opportunity to make choices that are socially responsible as well.

• Patronize Community Wealth Enterprises. Make an effort as a consumer to patronize Community Wealth Enterprises such as Newman's Own, Timberland, American Express, House of Seagram's, FILA, and others that have made major partnership commitments to nonprofit organizations.

• Use your skill or teach it. Find a school, community center, or nonprofit organization where you can teach or volunteer your skill.

• Demonstrate support for CWEs by writing or calling company officials to praise them for their community-building activities. In many cases they will be involved in difficult activities that have a reasonably high risk of failure. They need reinforcement. Hearing from you will be good for them and good for their employee morale.

• Take a sabbatical with a nonprofit or Community Wealth Enterprise. An in-depth, hands-on experience, whether three weeks or six months, provides an opportunity to see the work from their perspective, and for them to benefit from your skills.

• Write about your experience or find some other way to communicate it. Too many people still think that only government officials or professional social workers can make a difference. Volunteers should write op-eds or letters to the editor that provide firsthand personal accounts of how their own experiences have created community change and proven personally meaningful.

So how does one actually go about getting a wealth-creating enterprise started? Basically, by starting it. By crossing the line from idea to action. By putting a sign on the door and telling people it exists. This may sound both simplistic and obvious, but crossing this threshold from idea to action is far more difficult and far more important than all of the corporate bylaws, IRS forms, articles of incorporation, or solicitations for seed money that constitute the technical and legal necessities for beginning an organization. There are management books, videotapes, seminars, and consulting firms that specialize in providing advice on how to start a business, company, nonprofit organization, or association. They are produced by smart people. Their ideas are tested, tried, and true. Maybe you can afford them, maybe not. It doesn't matter. They are not for you. At least they are not for you *now*. Later such tools might provide insights to help you refine your ideas and practices. But if you are creating something because you need to, then trust that need.

Just as there is no one, single magic solution or silver bullet for solving the complex problems of hunger and poverty, there is no single formula or prescription for creating community wealth. Nor is there any substitute for the experimentation required to ensure your work will reflect your own original vision and passion. Every new idea must be brought to fruition in its own way. Genuine entrepreneurs don't copy, they invent. The photographer Harry Callahan, when asked why he never taught his art to student photographers, explained, "I felt so strongly that everybody had to find their own way. And nobody can teach you your own way. . . . For me, the thing about art is that it's always something strange. You're constantly breaking rules to try to get to something new. In terms of art the only real answer that I know of is to do it. If you don't do it, you don't know what might happen."

8

What I don't know is not as much of a problem
as what I am sure I know that just ain't so.

MARK TWAIN

Imagine a successful business whose revenues are over $30 million greater than the expenses incurred producing such revenues. It has never applied for or received government funding or government contracts. It has never borrowed money. It has no debt. It does not benefit from the interest income of a large endowment. It has forty-five paid employees with full health care benefits. It invests in mutual funds and money market funds and it retains agencies for consulting on design, marketing, training, and human resource issues. In the private sector such an enterprise would be seen for what it is—a sophisticated and profitable multimillion-dollar business.

But the description above is of Share Our Strength. It is not how most people would expect a nonprofit organization to be described. But such expectations and other widespread misconceptions about how nonprofits should work abound.

Share Our Strength does operate on a lean, no-frills budget, but that doesn't mean we don't pay good salaries to attract and retain good staff, and spend the money necessary to give them the tools and training they need to do their job. Such expenditures are not frills. Anything less would undermine our efforts, be wasteful of hard-earned donations and revenues, and in effect betray the confidence of our supporters.

Constructing a new approach to solving social problems through rebuilding community requires a new public understanding of the complexity of those problems and the sophistication of the solutions. Without greater public awareness, community nonprofits will find themselves trying to compete without the support necessary to attract resources.

Let's look at just a few of the common misperceptions that hinder nonprofit organizations from reaching their full potential.

The Best Nonprofits Are All Volunteer and Get Everything Donated.
This sounds great in theory but has severe disadvantages in practice that can best be summed up as "you get what you pay for." It's hard to wage a first-rate battle with second-rate materials. Used equipment breaks down more often than new equipment. Donated office space is frequently in a location where no

one wants to be, not just for aesthetic reasons, but for the practical reason that it is hard to do business there. Pro bono services such as legal counsel, accounting, design, and advertising can be incredibly valuable but not if paying customers are always being put ahead of your needs. Often donors want to give away surplus materials that may not match your needs. For example, food banks often get large quantities of sweetened cereals and diet soda that are not nutritious or good for the people they are trying to serve, but are donated because the manufacturers happened to have excess quantities of these products.

If you were about to start a new business, let's say a small innovative software company, would you try to get space in some run-down part of town donated for use as an office? Would you recruit volunteers instead of the most skilled and talented people available? Would you pay low salaries instead of compensation that could create an atmosphere of teamwork among the employees, who will feel invested in the venture for the long term? Would you save on administrative expenses by answering your own phones and copying and faxing your own materials? Would you forgo marketing and advertising and instead hope the public became aware of your work on its own? This is what is expected of nonprofit organizations fighting poverty in America today. It's a mentality that permeates much of the nonprofit community and has created a self-defeating atmosphere right from the start.

An organization is only as good as the people who run it. Whether it's the Walt Disney Company or Chrysler, City Year or the Children's Defense Fund, successful organizations require committed, stable, and secure leadership. Competitive salaries are one necessary ingredient. If you want skilled and trained people to stay, you need to pay them well. Why shouldn't they be? Does keeping kids out of gangs have less value to society than creating ads for soap or cigarettes? Is running an after-school program to tutor children of less value than handling litigation for a cable TV company? Some people think there's something inappropriate about being paid well to fight poverty, that maybe those funds would be better spent on poor people themselves. But this is a shortsighted attitude that envisions only short-term relief, not the building of an institution. In the long run poverty can be fought more effectively if the most qualified people are compensated at levels enabling them to afford to do it as long as necessary.

These are not perspectives heard often in the nonprofit world. Most nonprofits find it safer to be seen and not heard. Whether it is fear of retribution from cautious foundations or public opprobrium, too few nonprofits are willing to challenge the conventional wisdom about salaries and expenditures. These issues represent another important reason for nonprofits to become Community Wealth Enterprises and create their own wealth so that they have increased financial independence and can make expenditures where they are needed, even though they may not be popular. The nonprofit community itself must take responsibility for educating the contributing public. Unless we assume the burden of bringing a more sophisticated perspective to bear, then the nonprofit community will remain handcuffed to nineteenth-century notions that restrict their ability to accomplish anything as worthwhile as they otherwise could.

The Best Nonprofits Are Those with the Lowest Administrative Expenses and the Highest Percentage of Funds Going Directly to Program Support.

I would argue that the best nonprofits are those that are successful in accomplishing their mission. Impact and outcome should be the measuring sticks by which nonprofits are judged. An organization can have administrative overhead expenses lower than all the other organizations in the field, but if it's not accomplishing much, then what good is it?

I'm often asked by donors whether a portion of their contribution will be used to cover administrative costs. I dutifully explain that SOS has only a 6 percent administrative overhead, way below the national average. But what I want to say is: "You better hope so. Otherwise your check will just sit in a drawer and there won't be anyone to take it to the bank and deposit it. If you call to ask about it, there won't be anyone to answer the phone, either!" Administrative functions are crucial to running an organization in the most professional manner possible. Dollars that go toward paying postage, salaries, or staff benefits don't give a contributor the same warm feeling of satisfaction and accomplishment that buying a child a meal or a toy or building a classroom does. But costs such as these may be what enable an organization to operate, grow, and achieve its goals. Look at it this way: Have you ever decided not to buy a car because you thought too much of its sticker price would go toward paying executive salaries in Detroit or toward the cost of running the dealership? The truth is, you don't know what it costs to run the dealership or what it should cost. The judgment you are best qualified to make is whether the dealer's product meets your needs.

Obviously nonprofits should be as frugal and efficient as possible, but the issue should not be what percentage of funds go to fund-raising or administrative overhead costs. The issue should be whether the organization is fulfilling its mission as efficiently and as effectively as possible, and whether administrative expenditures further that mission or not. Nonprofits that want to be judged by this standard have a greater responsibility to make the public aware of the impact they are having and what their dollars are enabling the organization to accomplish. If an organization is clearly not demonstrating impact or effectiveness, then maybe it's not giving you good value for your dollar. Don't contribute. Make this the criterion by which you evaluate the recipient of your charitable support.

I Want to Earmark My Contribution for the Purchase of Food, Clothing, or Medicine for Someone Who Needs It.
But a nonprofit that feeds, clothes, and provides medicine for poor people usually doesn't need money to buy such items because they are donated. More often the challenge is in *getting* the items to the people who need them. For example, large food producers such as Kraft General Foods, Pillsbury, Nabisco, Dole, and Del Monte regularly and generously donate product that is not salable for mostly aesthetic reasons: food that's been mislabeled, has damaged packaging, or is too close to its expiration date. The organizations receiving this food need money for all of the expenses associated with getting that food to the people who need it, including transportation, refrigerated warehousing, computerized inventory, staffing, and outreach to the community in need so that people will be aware of the services available.

The Best Social Programs Put Children First.
You can't help a child without helping the child's parents. Children elicit more sympathy than absentee fathers and mothers on welfare. As a result, donors are more attracted to programs that identify children as their beneficiaries. But the 25 percent of children under the age of six who live below the poverty line do not

live alone. They are dependent upon their parents, grandparents, relatives, or caregivers, and cannot do well if those taking care of them aren't doing well, either.

Understandably the "adopt a child for just fifteen dollars a month" type of solicitation holds great appeal, but no amount of direct aid to a young child, assuming it reaches him, can succeed unless the child is in an environment where a caregiver—ideally a parent—nurtures, supports, teaches, disciplines, and trains him. A friend's pediatrician always said that the best thing a man could do for his child was to love its mother. The best thing that society can do for disadvantaged children is give their parents the support and services they need. In that sense, programs ranging from job training to adult literacy classes are social programs that help children.

Urgent Immediate Needs Make It Impossible to Invest and Plan for the Future.

A nonprofit that subscribes to this mentality is guaranteed to never be prepared for the future. When you're assisting people in circumstances as desperate as poverty, it is easy, as the cliché goes, to lose sight of the forest for the trees. But it is essential to maintain perspective.

If I were the CEO of any other business and had $3 million to $4 million available in liquid assets one week (the amount of cash on hand immediately following our Taste of the Nation events), only to spend that cash just a few weeks later, my board of directors would fire me for not investing at least some of that money wisely. Because of the pressure on nonprofits to provide emergency relief and assistance, they are almost never able to let their money make money—one of the most common and effective ways to increase resources. Like the man who never put aside money for a pension because he didn't think he could afford it, only to grow old and find himself poor, nonprofit organizations end up with fewer resources and help fewer people than they otherwise would if they had the strategic foresight and discipline to save and invest carefully.

For years after I left government, whenever I would bump into former colleagues or associates they would ask what I was now doing. I'd tell them about Share Our Strength, and, after listening politely, they would invariably ask, "So what else are you doing?" The answer of course was, "Nothing else, this is what I do," but the question was implicit with the assumption that nonprofit work by itself surely cannot be enough either to support you financially, challenge you intellectually, or fulfill you emotionally. It's time to recognize that entrepreneurial nonprofits that are managed professionally and create wealth can be the breeding ground for innovation and experimentation considered too risky for government, but essential to finding new approaches that government and community institutions can adopt. Those of us at the helm of nonprofit organizations must take the lead in challenging the conventional wisdom and antiquated methods that have slowed our progress toward a more prominent place in the national effort to rebuild community.

9

*No great cause is ever won or lost. The battle must always be
renewed and the creed restated. . . . For some things are
universal, catholic and undying. . . . These do not age or pass out
of fashion, for they symbolize eternal things. They are the
guardians of the freedom of the human spirit, the proof of what
our mortal frailty can achieve.*

> JOHN BUCHAN,
> *biographer of Montrose*

In the summer of 1993 my then-seven-year-old son Zachary
had a rare ear infection that required two weeks of painful
intravenous therapy. I had canceled all out-of-town trips
but was still working long hours. One Sunday afternoon the two
of us were in the car when he said, "Dad, can I ask you something?" In the past this has been a precursor to questions about
where babies come from or what happens to us when we die,
and other matters I invariably refer to his mother.

"Sure, what's up?" I replied, trying to disguise the hesitancy in my voice.

"What ... do ... you think ... is more important," he began, drawing each word out slowly as if he were searching carefully for the right ones, "feeding all of the hungry people or curing my disease?"

I explained that first of all he didn't have a disease, thank goodness, only a treatable infection, and second, he and his sister Mollie would always come first in terms of love and responsibility, but that it's also important to try to help other people if you can.

I thought about his question for a long time, though. Ultimately I convinced myself that he probably knew the answer despite a child's innate need to be explicitly reassured. But I also took it to be a question about how one finds the right balance between the abstract and the individual, between helping vast numbers of people in a massive national and international effort, while not neglecting to care for a single individual who might literally be within arm's reach, at the corner where you pick up your newspaper, on the subway, or lined up at the soup wagon beside the park.

One of my favorite *New Yorker* cartoons shows a pack of wolves late at night, straining their necks and raising their heads up toward the sky, baying at the moon with great anguish, as wolves do. One wolf says to the others, "My question is, are we having any impact?" It's a question I ask myself every day. Since SOS was founded, hunger and poverty have actually increased. The number of people seeking emergency food assistance at shelters and soup kitchens has skyrocketed. Neighborhoods have crumbled and communities have deteriorated. As much as we take pride in our ten-year history, the tens of millions of dollars distributed, and the thousands of volunteers we've deployed, it's easy for us to feel that we've been howling at a moon that has ignored us. But I don't believe that to be the case.

Our ten-year history has yielded two benefits: The first is that we've developed the organizational maturity to understand how to get the most bang for the buck, how to build a comprehensive and sophisticated grant-making strategy that encompasses emergency food assistance and support for longer-term efforts to prevent hunger. The second is that we've reached a level of financial resources that enables us to fund both immediate and long-term programs.

Each year SOS makes grants to nearly five hundred anti-hunger organizations in the United States and to international organizations working in about a dozen developing countries. We've distributed more than $25 million to date and will distribute another $25 million in the next two years alone. Counting grant recipients and adding up the number of dollars distributed, though, is not the same as measuring the impact those dollars have had. In many ways the methodology for measuring such impact doesn't yet exist. But careful research does permit us to know the effect of at least some of our dollars. We know for example that the thirty food rescue programs that received funds from SOS were able to increase the salvageable food they rescued, going from 18 million to 22 million pounds. We know that 27,000 children now have access to breakfast in school because of the twenty start-up grants and the forty-nine expansion grants we've awarded to school districts that will increase school breakfast participation by 25 percent.

Still, after ten years I search for and seize opportunities to renew my commitment and expand my understanding of the difficult work that engages us, to inspire us toward new growth, to sustain optimism, to fuel the revolution. One such opportunity presented itself recently as I flipped through a collection of Martin Luther King's speeches and came across an interview he gave to a rabbinical assembly on March 25, 1968—just ten days before he was killed.

"I was in Marks, Mississippi the other day and I found myself weeping before I knew it," he said. "I met boys and girls by the hundreds who didn't have any shoes to wear, who didn't have any food to eat in terms of three square meals a day, and I met their parents, many of whom don't even have jobs. I literally cried when I heard men and women saying that they were unable to get any food to feed their children."

Ten days later Dr. King was dead. It occurred to me that although there might be little else that distinguishes Marks from any other sleepy small town in the Mississippi delta, it was likely the place of Martin Luther King's last tears, tears shed more than twenty-five years ago, tears shed over hunger. That seemed reason enough to go.

❧

I found myself in a rental car driving through the Mississippi delta, the sun rising over fields of cotton and soybean that stretched as far as you could see. Single-engine crop dusters flew alongside, spraying, looping close enough to the car to make me scream, and spraying again.

When I thought about a small town circa 1968 I could visualize it only in black and white. But as I got closer I realized that it was 1994 and there were no more Mayberrys. There would probably be McDonald's franchises and Pizza Huts and Block-buster Videos. But I was wrong. Time hasn't stood still for the 1,723 people who live in Marks, Mississippi, but that's not for lack of trying. The cotton is high, the catfish are tasty, and the old-timers can sit on the porch and talk for hours. Marks is untouched. Many of the homes could still fit right into a vintage Walker Evans photograph. Narrow shoe-box shacks, trailers, and shanties. Broken-down cars, pickups and bicycles in the yards. Lots of dogs running loose.

There were some spectacular homes just on the other side of the Coldwater River and I asked Miss Lucy Turner, a seventy-two-year-old retired librarian, about them when I visited her in her living room on Maple Street, at the intersection of Peach and Pecan. "Cotton money. Those folks are quite wealthy. But that's not Marks across the river there; that's a suburb," she said without a trace of irony. "Thems are people that fled the inner city for better schools and such."

Miss Lucy Turner and other white residents constitute the minority population in Marks today and live in a still-uneasy tension with their black neighbors. She said to put her down as a "Doubting Thomas." "There's lot of families that when they met Dr. King they took their kids shoes away and had them run around on the street so he'd just think they were poor."

Miss Lucy knew of people I should talk to who were associated with Dr. King's visit. They weren't hard to find. Everyone seemed to live and work either across from the courthouse or next to the sheriff's office.

Everybody remembered Martin Luther King coming to town, but most remembered other visits of his, particularly those times when the press put Marks in the national spotlight, if only for a moment. The protest march of the mule train. Or the time Dr. King attended the funeral of a Mr. Phipps, who meant to accompany him on the march to Selma but dropped dead en route.

I went over to the office of the newspaper, *The Quitman County Democrat,* and asked the editor if they kept papers dating as far back as 1968.

The editor looked up from behind her cluttered desk in the front office. "We sure do. But they're pretty fragile," she warned. "What're you looking for anyway?"

"I'm interested in the times Martin Luther King came through town, especially March of 1968, just before he was killed"

"Well, we got the papers but you won't find nothing 'bout that," she said.

"Why not?"

"My daddy was the editor then. His theory at the time was: Ignore it long enough and hopefully it will just go away. He bought the paper in 1937. I've been editor since he died in '72. So I should know."

She did know. The back issues were kept across the street at the courthouse. The day after King came to town the front-page headline was "Mrs. June Sneed Wins Treasure Hunt." The Big 3 Lumber Company had sponsored a treasure hunt for the employees of Riverside Industries and Mrs. Sneed had correctly guessed that the treasure was in the trunk of Mrs. Murray's blue car. The story came complete with front-page photo of a confused-looking Mrs. Sneed being handed her prize: "a brand-new model 1200 Winchester pump shotgun with a 28-inch modified barrel."

It was a different time and place. Kroger had a half-page ad promoting catfish steaks for sixty-nine cents a pound and eggs for nine cents a dozen. There was a price war over whole fryers—twenty-seven cents at Krogers, twenty-nine cents at Tedford's. Kraft Mayo was selling at fifty-five cents a quart jar.

The paper also had front-page stories on the next meeting of the Boy Scout Leadership Council, the Marks Senior Class play *(One Foot in Heaven),* and even a column listing the schedule for picking up food stamps. There was not a single word about Martin Luther King's having been to town.

But contrary to the old editor's wishes, ignoring something doesn't make it go away, and that's as true for the conditions of poverty in Mississippi today as it was when King visited. Mississippi ranks fiftieth in child poverty rates by the American Public Health Association. It has the highest percentage of hungry people of any state in America—19.86 percent. Statistics available for nearby Humphries County, where SOS funds a community health advisers program, as it does in Quitman County, indicate that about half of the county's population lives below the poverty line. The infant mortality rate is 26.4 deaths per 1,000 live births, more than twice the too-high state rate of 12.2 per 1,000. Only 39 percent of the population have high school degrees. Less than 9 percent have college diplomas.

The poverty here is in many ways dramatic, but it is mostly heartbreakingly ordinary, endless, almost hopelessly passed on from generation to generation. Seventy to 80 percent of all of Quitman County's babies are born to teenage mothers. But they have to be delivered somewhere else. There's not one obstetrician in the county.

❦

My book of Dr. King's speeches quotes the rabbi who introduced him to the assembly that night in March of 1968.

"The politicians are astute, the establishment is proud, and the marketplace is busy," Rabbi Abraham Joshua Heschel began. "Placid, happy, merry, the people pursue their work, enjoy their leisure, and life is fair. People buy, sell, celebrate, and rejoice. They fail to realize that in the midst of our affluent cities there are districts of despair, areas of distress.

"Where does God dwell in America today? Is He at home with those who are complacent, indifferent to other people's agony, devoid of mercy? Is he not rather with the poor and the contrite in the slums?

"The situation of the poor in America is our plight, our sickness. To be deaf to their cry is to condemn ourselves."

The passage of time has only enhanced the pertinence of Rabbi Heschel's warning. People who are financially well off and have no contact with poverty are diminished by the poverty that entraps so many of those with whom they share this country. It may help explain the paradox of living in a period of sustained economic growth that also happens to be a period in which most people express a general unhappiness with the national state of affairs. Like a family with two healthy kids and a third who is desperately ill, part of the American family is seriously ailing, institutionalized in ghettos, on welfare, in public housing, victims of crime. In 1920, Agnes Repplier wrote in the *Atlantic Monthly,* "Things are as they are and no amount of self-deception makes them otherwise. . . . Somewhere in our hearts is a strong, though dimly understood, desire to face realities, and to measure consequences, to have done with the fatigue of pretending."

As a final resort my optimism may be nothing more than a faith in biology over experience. If compassion, common sense, and even self-interest don't work, perhaps biology will. If there is one thing that unites our species—black or white, rich or poor—it's the biological instinct to preserve and protect our off-spring, to keep them safe, to leave their generation better off than ours. Remember the child trapped in the well? How about the children trapped by drug dealers and handguns and poverty? Surely we can reach out to them with the same sense of urgency once we accept that the children in this country—all the children—are our own.

❧

I ended up talking to many people in Marks that day—so many that I missed the plane I was trying to catch. Driving back to the Memphis airport east on Highway 6, I realized that at the other end of the highway was Oxford, Mississippi, home to both Ole Miss and William Faulkner. I had plenty of time before the next flight and had always wanted to see Faulkner's home so I kept driving. It's tucked away in a beautiful, peaceful setting. I stood at the fence staring at it through the trees, thinking about that poor little town just down the highway, and taking hope from words Faulkner delivered when he won the Nobel Prize in 1949: "I believe that man will not only endure: he will prevail. He is immortal, not because he alone among creatures has an inexhaustible voice, but because he has a soul, a spirit capable of compassion and sacrifice and endurance."

10

Either we have hope within us or we don't, it is a dimension of the soul, and it's not essentially dependent on some particular observation of the world or estimate of the situation. . . . Hope, in this deep and powerful sense, is not the same as joy that things are going well or willingness to invest in enterprises that are obviously headed for early success, but rather, an ability to work for something because it is good, not just because it stands a chance to succeed. . . . Hope is definitely not the same thing as optimism. It is not the conviction that something will turn out well, but the certainty that something makes sense no matter how it turns out.

VÁCLAV HAVEL

When my father died in December of 1993, his brother's widow, my Aunt Lois, brought some old photographs to the funeral home to show me and my sister. She had taken it upon herself to become the family archivist, researching our family tree, collecting documents and pictures, and tape-recording oral histories.

My father's father had worked as a tailor and later, with my grandmother Rose, ran a small corner grocery store. Rose outlived my grandfather by about five years, and as a result I re-member her better than him—our Sunday-night visits to her dark home, her stories about marching in the streets to support the controversial presidential campaign of socialist candidate Eugene Debs, the frozen Hershey bars she always had in the freezer for my sister and me.

My grandfather died when I was just four years old, and I have only a hazy memory of him as a frail and very old man. He came to Ellis Island from Russia on the S.S. *Bonn,* a German shipping line, on August 16, 1911, as Israel Schorski. He was twenty-two years old.

My favorite photo of the batch that Aunt Louis brought was taken about three years earlier, maybe 1908. Six young soldiers of the czar's army are huddled around a desk somewhere in Russia. They can't be much older than twenty. Four are seated and two are standing. The men on each end are slightly older and mustached, looking like forbidding bookends. All are dressed smartly in starched, high-collared uniforms, their pants tucked into tall boots. A seriousness of purpose about this group is evident immediately. None are looking at the camera but each seems to wear an expression of hope and defiance. Taking a pic-ture in those days required one to sit still for the lengthy amount of time it took to get the exposure. The men were accommodat-ing but look anxious to get back to the business at hand.

Israel is seated on a cane-backed chair that is pulled up to a small writing desk, his posture erect, knees apart, and both feet flat on the floor. He is sitting forward somewhat, attentive, in a way that suggests something important is transpiring. The sol-dier next to him has an arm around his shoulder in a demon-stration of camaraderie, but he is not looking at Israel. Instead, he and the other four soldiers are staring intently at a book Israel is holding open, making my grandfather the focal point of the photo. Another book, closed, sits on the desk. Nothing else can be made out in the background, no clues as to where they are. That may be as they wished it. Once a week these men would secretly meet to publish an underground newspaper in defiance of the czar. Like many in Russia at that time, they shared ideas about freedom. They knew that such ideas had power. And they acted on that knowledge. They knew that ideas are borne aloft in the words used to express them and that such words inspire people, motivate people, organize ordinary people into a force greater than just the sum of their parts.

One of the world's great revolutions was brewing in Russia. Neither Israel nor his five co-conspirators were its heroes, but they were every bit as much a part of it. Who can know the impact of six ordinary men? Who can know how many and which acts of idealism and resistance and courage it takes to inch an idea over the edge from dream to reality? Can history ever know with certainty which were consequential and which were not? This is what I thought about while staring at the photos my aunt brought to my father's funeral. And as I looked into Israel's gentle but intense eyes it was a moment before I realized that they were mine.

❧

Journeys often end where they began and sometimes I feel as though mine has come full circle. As I've traveled the country on behalf of Share Our Strength, making hundreds of visits to more than thirty-five states over the past two years, the overwhelming, unavoidable sensation is that of a campaign. The speeches, the endless fund-raising, the interviews, the events, the thank-you notes to large donors, the need to motivate and sustain volunteers, the effort to identify the right organizer who will represent that all-important first concentric circle. Sometimes I even find myself speaking in the same hotel ballroom where Gary Hart addressed a Democratic Mayors Conference or checking into the same Holiday Inn that was our command post before a midwestern primary. I experience a strange sense of déjà vu, but in a way it reassures me that I'm doing something I've long prepared to do.

One of my more ambitious hopes for this book is that it sets off something of a debate, that it gets people talking, arguing, and discussing new ideas. There is much this book will leave unanswered. And over time some of its ideas may be proven to be wrong. But I want its readers—liberal or conservative, political or non-political—to see it as a challenge to sharpen their own ideas and put them out there for discussion. The political environment in this country is so unforgiving that most people are more comfortable rallying around consensus ideas of the lowest common denominator than they are taking risks on behalf of innovative, unorthodox concepts.

Without a doubt, our greatest challenge is to make people care again about alleviating the effects of poverty, to make them want to do something about it in the first place, and to make them feel that they can. Young people in America today grow up assuming that hunger, homelessness, and poverty are the norm. They have not experienced the alternative. A freshman entering college or a high school graduate enlisting in the navy has likely never in his or her lifetime walked down the streets of a major American city without uncomfortably stepping around homeless men, mothers, or Vietnam vets sitting beside the cardboard signs that advertise their plight. The scene is sad but it is no longer shocking.

Having worked in and around Washington for nearly twenty years, it is remarkable to me that the number of occasions I've had to cross the Anacostia River into the impoverished southeast quadrant of the city can be counted on one hand. Using only thumbs. One of the most insidious aspects of poverty in America today is that it is confined to places most Americans need not see, drive through, experience, or touch. We may think we've seen something of it because of the homeless people we pass on our way to work, but they are poverty's dark shadow more than they are poverty itself.

If we are to be moved away from apathy and despair, we must be convinced that there is a better vision to be attained. The task is made harder by the fact that we are living in an era that does not have its Martin Luther King or Bobby Kennedy, James Baldwin or even Joan Baez, an era without a voice of fire and passion and eloquence. The moving cadences of the 1960s, delivered before vast throngs at historic moments—at the Lincoln Memorial, in South Africa, before a tense crowd in Indianapolis—have been replaced by the clipped and clever sound bites that guarantee fifteen minutes of fame from the cool, clean studios of "Larry King Live" or "Good Morning America."

But this may not be as discouraging as it sounds. As strong an influence as stirring words can have (and as badly as they are missed by those of us who grew up in the 1960s), stirring deeds can matter even more. Is there anything more noble than responding to John Kennedy's challenge to "ask what you can do for your country" or to any other famed call of society's moral conscience? Perhaps there is. Perhaps it is acting even in the absence of such a summons. Ours is an organization of ordinary people taking such actions every day. People putting food in front of others who have no access to food. People leaving their homes or offices and driving into neighborhoods where there are no such homes or offices but people there that they can teach, train, and befriend. People using their restaurants, hotels, public relations firms, printing companies, photography darkrooms, or breweries to produce the dollars needed to staff kitchens, shelters, and health clinics. Most would never consider themselves political activists in any sense of the word, nor would they be rigidly tied to one ideology or another. As the heroes of the generation before them were those who demonstrated for civil rights, perhaps the heroes of our generation will be those who are demonstrating their own civil responsibilities.

In the end, revitalizing our democracy depends upon revitalizing ourselves. The new language of community that America longs for can't be legislated, mandated, or purchased. It can be given voice only by an unprecedented chorus of citizen action.

There is a rich historical and philosophical context to the definition of civil society and civic duty. It originates with Plato and runs through Jefferson as an indispensable element of democracy. What we are trying to do today is impossible—run a modern democracy without one of its principle ingredients, namely civic engagement. It is not an option or a luxury. It is a necessity. A new strategy for sharing strength and creating community wealth can make it a reality. It can restore our nation's ability to reimagine possibility and dream once more of all that a truly great America can be.

RESOURCE DIRECTORY

*A sampling of national and community-based organizations that
strengthen communities across the country*

NATIONAL ORGANIZATIONS

ALLIANCE FOR NATIONAL RENEWAL
1445 Market St., Suite 300
Denver, CO 80202
(303) 571-4343
*Connects grassroots activist organizations focused on similar issues to help
them share ideas and strategies through newsletters and publications.*

BEST BUDDIES INTERNATIONAL
1325 G St., NW, Suite 500
Washington, DC
(202) 347-7265
*Establishes one-to-one friendships between mentally retarded individuals and
community members.*

BLACK STUDENT LEADERSHIP NETWORK
25 E St., NW
Washington, DC 20001
(202) 662-3515
*Coordinated nationally by the Children's Defense Fund, BSLN is a group of
African-American college students aged eighteen to thirty who network
among grassroots organizations in communities nationwide, with the goal of
empowering a new generation of community-service leaders.*

BREAD FOR THE WORLD
1100 Wayne Ave., #1000
Silver Spring, MD 20910
(301) 608-2400
A Christian citizens' movement against hunger, BFW advocates on behalf of hungry people worldwide, gives technical assistance to congregations and grassroots anti-hunger organizations, generates media attention for hunger and poverty issues, and through Bread for the World Institute, publishes original research.

BREAK AWAY
Vanderbilt University
Box 6026, Station B
Nashville, TN 37235
(615) 343-0385
Matches college groups with local nonprofits to provide "alternative" spring breaks focused on volunteering and community service.

CAMPUS OUTREACH OPPORTUNITY LEAGUE (COOL)
1101 15th St., NW, Suite 203
Washington, DC 20005
(202) 637-7004
A national organization that supports and promotes college student involvement in community service and social action through conferences, programs, training, and consulting with more than 700 campuses nationwide.

CENTER FOR COMMUNITY CHANGE
1000 Wisconsin Ave., NW
Washington, DC 20007
(202) 342-0519
Provides technical assistance to more than 250 low-income minority groups nationwide, helping grassroots organizations get the organizing tools they need to better their neighborhoods and revitalize their communities through economic development.

**CENTER ON HUNGER, POVERTY AND NUTRITION POLICY AT TUFTS
UNIVERSITY**
11 Curtis Ave.
Medford, MA 02155
(617) 627-3956
*Works to eliminate domestic hunger and enrich policy discussions on ways to
protect children and their families through research, policy analysis, technical
assistance, and education.*

CHILDREN'S DEFENSE FUND
25 E St., NW
Washington, DC 20001
(202) 628-8787
*A nonprofit research and advocacy organization that exists to provide a strong
and effective voice for the children of America, who cannot vote, lobby, or
speak out for themselves. CDF focuses primarily on the needs of poor,
minority, and disabled children, and works to promote preventive investment
in them.*

CITIZEN SCHOOLS
c/o Paul A. Dever School
325 Mt. Vernon St.
Dorchester, MA 02125
(617) 635-8694
*Provides educational apprenticeships taught by community volunteers for
nine- to thirteen-year-olds, primarily from low-income families, during
summers and after-school hours.*

CITY CARES OF AMERICA
1737 H St., NW
Washington, DC 20006
(202) 887-0500
*Network of city-based volunteer service organizations that engage volunteers
and corporate teams to participate in service projects in their communities.*

CITY YEAR
11 Stillings St.
Boston, MA 02210
(617) 350-0700
An Americorps program, City Year is a national service organization which unites young adults aged seventeen to twenty-three for a demanding year of full-time community service, leadership development, and civic engagement.

CORPORATION FOR NATIONAL SERVICE
1201 New York Ave., NW
Washington, DC 20525
(202) 606-5000
Through its three main programs, AmeriCorps, Learn and Serve, and Senior Service Corps, the Corporation for National Service engages people of all ages and backgrounds in service to their communities and is a resource for service opportunities nationwide.

FIRST BOOK
1319 F St., NW, Suite 604
Washington, DC 20004
(202) 393-1222
A national nonprofit organization committed to giving disadvantaged children their first new book and continued support. First Book targets its support toward children and families in need and promotes literacy and family skills.

FOOD RESEARCH AND ACTION CENTER (FRAC)
1875 Connecticut Ave., NW, Suite 540
Washington, DC 20009
(202) 986-2200
Works at the national and state level to improve public policies to eradicate hunger and under-nutrition in the United States. FRAC is a nonprofit and nonpartisan research, public-policy, and legal center that serves as a national anti-hunger network for thousands of community groups and individuals nationwide.

HandsNet
20195 Stevens Creek Blvd., Suite 120
Cupertino, CA 95014
(408) 257-4500
*An on-line computer service that connects more than 3,000 human-service
organizations, HandsNet links nonprofits with shared interests and posts
relevant reports, congressional testimony, legislative updates, media alerts, and
technical assistance to these organizations and their networks.*

Homeless Empowerment Relationship Organization (HERO)
2302 Laper, Suite H
Flint, MI 48503
(810) 239-3089
*Designed by those it serves, HERO recruits homeless adults from shelters and
substance-abuse programs and connects them with community volunteers who
help their partners set and reach goals, including permanent housing, jobs, and
education.*

"I Have a Dream" Foundation
330 Seventh Ave., 20th floor
New York, NY 10001
(212) 293-5480
*Targets at-risk students and pays the college tuition of students who graduate
from high school, and provides comprehensive tutoring, mentoring, family
counseling, and extracurricular activities.*

Local Initiatives Support Corporation (LISC)
733 Third Ave.
New York, NY 10017
(212) 455-9800
*National nonprofit that supports local Community Wealth Enterprises across
the country in their efforts to improve low-income housing. Provides fiscal and
technical assistance to help people revitalize their neighborhoods and incite
business and commercial development.*

RESOURCE DIRECTORY

NETWORKING IN THE PUBLIC INTEREST/COMMUNITY JOBS
30 Irving Pl., 9th floor
New York, NY 10003
(212) 475-1001
Publishes ACCESS: The National Service Guide, which lists service corps, volunteer centers, and resources for finding jobs and internships in the nonprofit sector. Offers information on volunteer and community-service organizations nationwide.

ONE HUNDRED BLACK MEN
105 East 22nd St.
New York, NY
(212) 777-7070
Founded in 1965, this civic organization has more than 500 members from business, professional, and political sectors working to achieve meaningful gains for blacks in housing, education, employment, health services, and public policies.

PLAYING TO WIN NETWORK
Education Development Center
55 Chapel St.
Newton, MA 02158
(617) 969-7101 x 2727
Supports organizations who provide and promote access to computer technologies for underserved populations.

PUBLIC ALLIES
1511 K St., NW, Suite 330
Washington, DC
(202) 638-3300
Places young people committed to careers in community service with nonprofits and trains them to be tomorrow's community leaders.

ROCK THE VOTE
1460 4th St., Suite 200
Santa Monica, CA 90401
(310) 656-2464
Educates and empowers young people to register to vote and to speak out on issues that affect their lives.

Rural Coalition
851 North Madison St.
Arlington, VA 22205
(703) 534-1845
*Works to meet the nutrition and health needs of low-income rural
populations, especially farm workers and rural minorities.*

Second Harvest
116 S. Michigan Ave., #4
Chicago, IL 60603
(312) 263-2303
*The largest charitable source of food in America, Second Harvest is a
nationwide network of 185 food banks, supplying more than 40,000 local
pantries, soup kitchens, homeless shelters, and other nonprofit agencies.*

Share Our Strength
1511 K St., NW, Suite 940
Washington, DC 20005
(202) 393-2925
*Mobilizes industries and individuals to contribute their talents to fight hunger.
SOS awards grants to more than 800 organizations in the United States,
Canada, and the developing world that work to alleviate hunger now and
prevent hunger in the long term. More than 10,000 chefs, restaurateurs,
writers, business leaders, and concerned individuals contribute their skills to
SOS's creative fund-raising, community outreach, direct service, and public
education programs, helping SOS broaden awareness and support for the
cause.*

Student Coalition for Action in Literacy Education (SCALE)
School of Education, UNC-CH
140½ E. Franklin St., CB # 3505
Chapel Hill, NC 27599-3505
(919) 962-1542
*Mobilizes and trains college students to form campus-based literacy projects.
Run by current students and recent college graduates, SCALE offers technical
assistance and training, holds conferences, and has projects on more than forty
campuses nationwide.*

TEACH FOR AMERICA
One World Trade Center, 78th floor
New York, NY 10048
(800) 832-1230
The National Teacher Corps of talented, dedicated recent college graduates who commit two years to teach in urban and rural public schools, which traditionally suffer from teacher shortages. TFA is an Americorps program.

WHO CARES MAGAZINE
1511 K St., NW, Suite 1042
Washington, DC 20005
(202) 628-1691
A nonprofit magazine that highlights service opportunities and social action nationwide. The magazine features youth-led nonprofit initiatives and sponsors topical forums to spur dialogue and to educate, challenge, and inspire future community leaders.

YOUTH SERVICE AMERICA
1101 15th St., NW, Suite 200
Washington, DC 20005
(202) 296-2992
A national organization that provides policy and leadership development, technical assistance, and training to programs and organizations that support, promote, and encourage national and community service.

COMMUNITY-BASED ORGANIZATIONS

APPALACHIAN WOMEN'S GUILD
P.O. Box 1026
Tracy City, TN 37387
(615) 592-8558
Provides education, training, and emergency food assistance to low-income women in rural Tennessee. Training includes computer skills, literacy, job skills, and referrals to social services.

CHILDREN'S HEALTH FUND
317 East 64th St.
New York, NY 10021
(212) 535-9400
With mobile medical units, CHF brings medical and nutrition services to indigent children in inner-city and rural communities across the United States.

FEDERATION OF SOUTHERN COOPERATIVES
100 Edgewood Ave., Suite 814
Atlanta, GA 30303
(404) 524-6882
Builds economic strength among rural, high-need communities by creating markets for low-income farmers to sell their produce, and for rural small businesses to sell their products.

FIFTH AVENUE COMMITTEE
199 14th St.
Brooklyn, NY, 11215
(718) 965-2777
Creates community-based businesses, develops low-income housing, facilitates low-income tenant ownership, and promotes community and tenant organizing to provide neighborhood residents with economic opportunities and adequate housing.

FIRST NATIONS DEVELOPMENT INSTITUTE
The Stores Building, 11917 Main St.
Fredericksburg, VA 22408
(703) 371-5615
Awards grants to Native-led projects focusing on health, nutrition, and economic development in Indian communities.

FUNDS FOR THE COMMUNITY'S FUTURE
1133 15th St., NW, Suite 605
Washington, DC 20005
(202) 331-0592
Enables low-income neighborhoods to provide scholarships for college or secondary education to their own youth by establishing neighborhood accounts funded through student-run community service and neighborhood-based fundraising projects.

L.A. COALITION TO END HOMELESSNESS
1010 S. Flower, Suite 216
Los Angeles, CA 90015
(213) 746-6511
In partnership with the Interfaith Hunger Coalition, established a model Hunger Organizing Project to train more than 600 low-income people to lead grassroots anti-hunger and anti-poverty campaigns and become anti-hunger advocates.

MARY'S CENTER FOR MATERNAL AND CHILD CARE
2333 Ontario Rd., NW
Washington, DC 20009
(202) 483-8196
Offers medical and nutrition services, preventive health care, translation, and access to social services to low-income Latino women and their children.

MINNESOTA CLIENTS COUNCIL/DULUTH TENANTS UNION
206 West 4th St., Room 212
Duluth, MN 55806
(218) 722-6808
Prepares low-income people to challenge systems and standards that impede their access to higher-wage jobs, affordable food, and safe and affordable housing.

MISSOURI RURAL CRISIS CENTER
710 Rangeline St.
Columbia, MO 65201
(314) 449-1336
Provides sustainable agriculture education and advocacy work, and conducts outreach to rural and urban churches and community organizations to bring produce to inner-city areas.

NATIONAL COUNCIL OF NEGRO WOMEN
P.O. Box 56
Lexington, MS 39095
(601) 834-1676
Provides emergency assistance for single-parent households with elderly family members or young children in need.

OPERATION GET DOWN
9980 Gratiot
Detroit, MI 48213
(313) 921-9422
Through a combination of food assistance, case management, and skills training, Operation Get Down enables community residents to learn from each other and work toward economic self-reliance.

PROJECT BREAD
11 Beacon St., Suite 800
Boston, MA 02108
(617) 723-5000
Works to improve nutrition among poor children through public outreach, community action, and advocacy aimed at increasing children's participation in federal nutrition programs.

PROJECT M.A.N.A.
P.O. Box 3980
Incline Village, NV 89450
(702) 831-6080
Works to empower hundreds of low-income Hispanic families through in-home nutrition education, nutrition workshops, and community outreach.

RHEEDLEN CENTERS FOR CHILDREN AND FAMILIES
2770 Broadway
New York, NY 10025
(212) 866-0700
An innovative network of neighborhood-based groups aimed at serving at-risk inner city youth through violence prevention, after-school care, and family education.

RURAL ORGANIZING AND CULTURAL CENTER
103 Swinney Lane
Lexington, MS 39095
(601) 834-3080
Offers comprehensive services to low-income rural residents, including gardening projects, nutrition education, and cooking classes for youth and teen parents to promote good nutrition.

ABOUT THE AUTHOR

From 1978 through 1987, Bill Shore worked on the Senate and presidential campaign staffs of Senator Gary Hart in a variety of capacities, including legislative director and political director. From 1990 to 1992, he served as chief of staff for Senator Robert Kerrey. Currently the executive director of Share Our Strength, Shore founded the organization in 1984. He is the editor of a number of anthologies, including *Louder Than Words, Voices Louder Than Words, Writers Harvest, Mysteries of Life and the Universe,* and *The Nature of Nature,* whose proceeds benefit Share Our Strength hunger-relief programs. He lives outside Washington, D.C., with his wife, Bonnie, and children Zach and Mollie.